Home Safety

Handbook

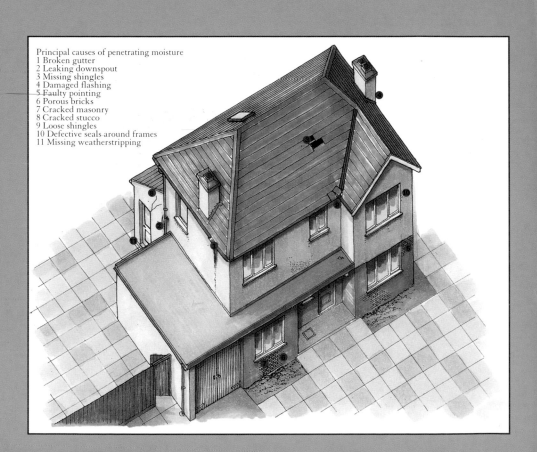

Principal causes of penetrating moisture
1 Broken gutter
2 Leaking downspout
3 Missing shingles
4 Damaged flashing
5 Faulty pointing
6 Porous bricks
7 Cracked masonry
8 Cracked stucco
9 Loose shingles
10 Defective seals around frames
11 Missing weatherstripping

Popular
Mechanics

Home
Safety
Handbook

Practical Tips
for Safe Living

Nancy J. Becker

HEARST BOOKS
A Division of Sterling Publishing Co., Inc.
New York

Popular Mechanics Home Safety Handbook
Practical Tips for Safe Living

Design: Alexandra Maldano
Cover Design: Celia Fuller
Copy Editor: Bruce Macomber

Safety Note: Homes built prior to 1978 may have
been constructed with hazardous materials: lead and
asbestos. You can test painted surfaces with a test kit
available at most hardware stores. Asbestos can be
found in ceiling and wall materials, joint compound,
insulation, and flooring. Hire a professional,
licensed hazardous-removal company to check for
this and remove any hazardous materials found

Published by Hearst Books
A Division of Sterling Publishing Co., Inc.
387 Park Avenue South, New York, NY 10016

Popular Mechanics is a trademark owned by Hearst
Magazines Property, Inc., in USA, and Hearst
Communications, Inc., in Canada. Hearst Books is a
trademark owned by Hearst Communications, Inc.

www.popularmechanics.com

Distributed in Canada by Sterling Publishing
c/o Canadian Manda Group, 165 Dufferin Street
Toronto, Ontario, Canada M6K 3H6

Distributed in Australia by Capricorn Link
(Australia) Pty. Ltd.
P.O. Box 704, Windsor, NSW 2756 Australia

Manufactured in China

ISBN 1-58816-457-8

Library of Congress Cataloging-in-Publication Data
Becker, Nancy J. (Nancy Jane), 1956-
  Popular Mechanics home safety handbook :
practical tips for safe living / Nancy J. Becker.
     p. cm.
  Includes index.
  ISBN 1-58816-457-8
  1. Home accidents--Prevention. I. Title: Home
safety handbook. II. Title.
  TX150.B43 2005
  643'.028'9--dc22
                                        2004019787

10 9 8 7 6 5 4 3 2 1

Contents

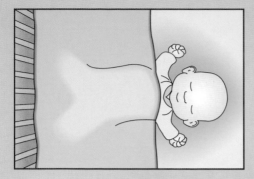

Introduction

As we hurry through our busy lives, we often find ourselves reacting to events rather than controlling the conditions that cause them to occur. The continuing complexity of engagement in the world means that much will happen, good and bad, to us and around us. It's a dynamic, sometimes dangerous world; there is much to consider, perhaps even to fear.

It is perhaps ironic that the greatest threats to human well-being today are those that have threatened us in the past, most of which are simply, and logically, preventable. Traffic accidents; smoke from fire; falls; accidental poisoning; drowning or suffocation - are the mishaps that most often lead to injury or death. However, with a little forethought and planning these injuries and deaths could be greatly diminished and perhaps prevented, particularly in the controlled environ of the home.

Living safely requires knowledge and time. You must educate yourself about some of the simple steps that you can take to prevent accidents from happening. Some of these steps involve ways of thinking and acting; some involve physical changes in the layout of the household; others involve planning for an accident the very act of which may prevent it from occurring in the first place. All this takes time, but is time well spent.

For example, experts agree that smoke detectors save lives. Every floor of the home, every kitchen, and every landing outside bedrooms should have a working smoke detector, the batteries for which should be tested monthly and changed once a year. Smoke detectors are inexpensive, simple devices that no home should be without.

Consider taking a CPR (cardiopulmonary resuscitation) course and learn the Heimlich maneuver, a method for saving a choking victim. Of course every home should have a well-stocked first aid-kit and everyone in the family should know where to find it.

People have been advised for years to post emergency phone numbers; today they can be programmed into most phones for instant dialing. Cell phones offer instant access to assistance as well as the ability to communicate if land lands go down. Caregivers should carry a cell phone at all times.

While there are growing concerns over the prospect of calamitous world events, statistics show that when it comes to health and safety we would be better off concentrating on issues closer to home. Obesity, particularly among children, and environmental tobacco smoke pose very real dangers to health and longevity; both are eminently controllable.

Take the time to learn about safety in the home. Get family members involved in the process by talking about and rehearsing basic safety practices. The time and effort you put forth today will be well worth it. You can bet your life on it.

—James Meigs
EDITOR-IN-CHIEF
Popular Mechanics

Safeguard

1

ing Infants and Children

Introduction

Babies and children depend on the adults in their lives to keep them safe. While every parent or guardian probably envisions the home as a safe harbor for the family, houses and apartments provide the setting for most injuries to and accidental deaths of people of any age.

The objects that we live with and use every day are potentially dangerous whether used incorrectly or, in some cases, used exactly as designed. While there are many ways to protect children from injury through awareness and the safe use of household objects, the single most important thing that we can do is to simply be present. Nothing can take the place of on-site adult supervision.

That being said, the home is an intriguing new terrain for babies and toddlers and must be considered anew on their arrival. Objects, textures, substances, and places in the home quite ordinary to the adult present certain hazards to babies and children. The time taken to "babyproof" your home may mean the difference between safety and harm to those you love.

Although countless safety devices are available for the home, consider carrying a cell phone. Particularly helpful in places such as the bathroom, the backyard, or poolside, cell phones allow you to provide supervision without ever leaving the area to make a call for assistance.

Cell phones make it easier for you to stay with your children and can provide instant access to help.

Crib Safety

The safest crib is a new one. Look for a crib bearing a label certifying that it meets the U.S. Consumer Product Safety Commission's standards in crib design and manufacture. Here are other important considerations when buying or maintaining a crib:

▲ Vertical slats on cribs should have no more than 2⅜" of space between them.

STRUCTURE

There should be no more than 2⅜ inches of space between the vertical crib slats in order to prevent the baby's head from becoming stuck.

The 4 corner posts must be the same height as, or less than ⅟₁₆ of an inch higher than, the end panels to prevent catchpoints for baby's clothing.

Neither headboard nor footboard should contain cutouts where a baby's head could become lodged.

While antique cribs look charming, they may contain dangerous cutouts, irregular spacing, or even lead paint. Lead paint was used until 1978. Avoid antique and used cribs.

HARDWARE

A crib's hardware should be checked frequently. Tighten loose screws and bolts. Careful attention should be paid to the

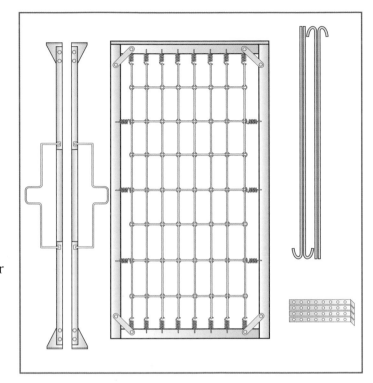

▲ Make sure that that mattress support hangers are firmly secured.

mattress support hangers and the hooks to which they are attached. Either of these pieces can break or dislodge, creating a space in which a baby can be trapped.

A child should not be able to drop the side of the crib. Check the dropside releases to ensure that two separate motions, or a single motion with a minimum force of ten pounds, are required to release the side.

MATTRESS

The mattress should fit tightly within the crib. No gaps should exist between the mattress and the sides or top and bottom of the crib. If you can insert two fingers between the mattress and the crib surrounding it, the mattress is too small.

Choose a firm, flat mattress and do not layer soft bedding, quilts, or comforters in the crib; they can suffocate a child.

Plastic bags should never be used as mattress covers or be used anywhere near a crib.

As soon as an infant can stand in the crib, the mattress should be placed at its lowest level, and when a child reaches a height of 35 inches, she has outgrown the crib.

SHEETS AND LINEN

Use only fitted bottom sheets designed specifically for cribs that stay securely over the mattress edges. Do not use sheets that pull away easily from the corners, and never use adult-sized sheets in a crib.

Do not use heavy or adult-sized blankets or quilts, and never place pillows in the crib.

SLEEPWEAR

The Consumer Product Safety Commission recommends that a child's sleepwear be either flame-resistant or snug-fitting to prevent burn injury from fire. Parents and caregivers should look for tags on infant sleepwear that indicate that it is flame-resistant. If not, the garment should fit snugly. Loose-fitting clothing more easily ignites and burns..

CRIB TOYS

Do not place large stuffed animals and toys in the crib. They can suffocate an infant or be used as a means for the child to climb from the crib and should be avoided.

Mobiles should be beyond the reach of a child and removed altogether when the child is able to sit up. Avoid homemade mobiles instead choose store-bought models that meet current safety standards.

Wall decorations featuring ribbons or strings should never be hung within reach of a child's crib as they pose the risk of entanglement or strangulation.

Sudden Infant Death Syndrome (SIDS)

Although the causes of sudden infant death syndrome are not known, the American Academy of Pediatrics, Task Force on Infant Sleep Position and Sudden Infant Death Syndrome (March 2000), made the following recommendations that may reduce the risk of SIDS:

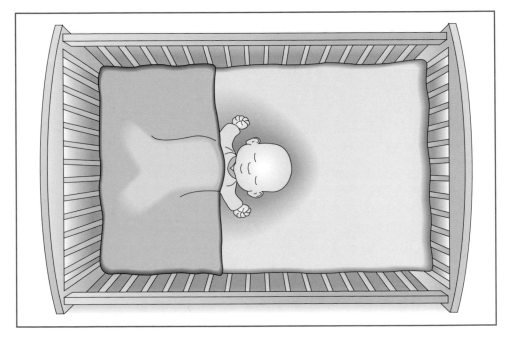

▲ Baby should be placed on her back to sleep.

■ Place your baby on her back to sleep.

■ Eliminate environmental tobacco smoke (secondhand smoke) exposure to your baby.

■ Avoid the use of soft bedding material in the crib such as comforters, quilts, or large, thick blankets.

■ Do not overheat your baby's room or overdress her. Pediatricians generally recommend a room temperature of between 68 and 70 degrees.

Structural Dangers in the Home

WINDOWS

The quality of home life is vastly improved by the light and air that windows admit, but a home with infants and children forces its occupants to look at windows more critically. Although supervision is the most important factor in preventing household accidents, a fall from a window can happen in seconds, perhaps the second it takes to answer a ringing phone or even turn to address another child. Windows on the ground level still warrant consideration since what seems a harmless few feet to an adult can mean serious injury or even death to an infant or toddler.

The windows in homes with babies, toddlers, and children should always be closed and locked or secured by window guards or stops. There are really no exceptions to this rule. Screens designed to keep insects out are not manufactured to keep children in and should not be presumed safe. As soon as a baby is mobile, crawling or playing around windows or sliding glass doors should be forbidden.

The area around a window should be clear and free of furniture to prevent a child from climbing near the window. A window open only a few inches will likely get the attention of your inquisitive toddler.

AIR CONDITIONERS

Never assume that the installation of an air-conditioning unit makes a window safe. The accordion gate designed to close off the open portion of the window can be easily penetrated by a child as young as two or three. Reinforce the accordion plastic with a panel of plywood that is screwed securely to the window frame.

WINDOW GUARDS

Window guards are metal gates permanently fixed to the windowsill that prevent passage through the bottom half of an open window. Consider the following when installing window guards in the home.

Ensure proper installation of window guards by consulting your local fire department, building code official, or building superintendent.

Window guards can prevent passage in the event of a fire, a fact that should be considered when planning a fire-escape route.

Contact an organization such as the U.S. Consumer Product Safety Commission (www.cpsc.gov) to determine whether the product meets current safety standards.

▲ Grills or guards should be placed on all windows.

A dult supervision can prevent accidents involving infants and children.

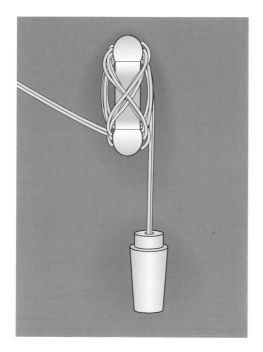

WINDOW COVERINGS

The cords on draperies, blinds, or other window treatments are potentially hazardous. They can become wrapped around a child's neck and cause strangulation. Never leave long or dangling cords within a child's reach. Although cords that contain no looped ends pose less risk, cords or rope of any kind are dangerous if within arm's reach. Be particularly vigilant about window treatments near a crib or child's bed. Your child should never be able to reach up and "play" with the cord.

GARAGE DOORS WITH AUTOMATIC OPENERS

Think back to the games you invented as a child and you might be able understand the "thrill" of a game entitled "Beat the garage door." The object of the game is to run underneath the door before it has a chance to close. While thrilling to children, the game should be met with alarm from adults. Kids have been struck by the descending door or even trapped beneath it, and injury or death have been the result.

Adult supervision can go a long way in preventing such

▲ The cords and pulls of window blinds are a potential strangling hazard for infants and children.

mishaps. Children should be taught not to play in or around the garage unless an adult is present. The U.S. Consumer Product Safety Commission (CPSC) also recommends that the garage-door remote control be locked in the glove compartment of the car and that the wall-mounted switch inside the garage be installed beyond the reach of children.

It is important that garage-door openers contain an automatic reverse mechanism in the event that the door comes into contact with a person or object when closing. Such safety-reverse features automatically stop and reverse the direction of the door when it comes into contact with any object.

▼ Never allow children to play around garage doors.

All garage-door openers offered for sale in the United States since 1993 must include an external entrapment protection system, according to the CPSC. Many include an electric eye or sensor that stops and reverses the closing garage door if an object moves under the door and breaks the infrared beam.

Door openers sold prior to 1993 should be inspected for balance (i.e., door will maintain any position to which it has been opened) and reversibility.

MANUAL GARAGE DOORS

A garage door that is opened and closed by hand must be operated with care; once again adult supervision is called for. Injuries to the hands or feet may occur as a result of the speed with which the door closes, as well as its weight. Fingers can be caught in the closing panels or the door hardware.

Whether your home has an automatic or manually operated garage door, the CPSC recommends inspection of the door and its hardware every 30 days. Children should be instructed that garage doors are not playthings and must be operated by an adult.

ELECTRICITY

Outlet Covers

New parents are often told to get down on their hands and knees and crawl around the living room to see the world from the eye level of their new arrival. From such a vantage point it's easy to see why a toddler would be drawn to electrical sockets: they're right at eye level! Inherently curious, children like nothing better than fitting one small object into another.

Block all unused electrical sockets with outlet covers to prevent electrocution. Make sure the covers are not easily removed by probing fingers and are large enough to prevent being put in the mouth.

▲ Outlet covers can prevent children from coming into contact with electrical currents.

Power Cords

To a toddler or infant learning to pull herself up, a power cord can look like a lifeline. Don't let power cords dangle where a child can pull on them. Use furniture to block or hide electrical cords—for example, run a lamp or computer cord behind a bed or desk—and avoid using extension cords with lamps or appliances. Tie excess cord into bundles and hide out of reach.

FURNITURE

Furniture Can Tip Over

Who would guess that something as innocuous as a chest of drawers could pose a danger to toddlers and children? But children are the majority of victims treated in the United States annually for accidents involving furniture, according to the Consumer Product Safety Commission.

Bookshelves, bureaus, desks, and stands can tip over and fall on a child, particularly when they are used as a means for the child to reach for something or to pull herself up. Drawers can act as enticing yet dangerous steps for a toddler attempting to reach a toy on a bureau's top.

TO PREVENT TIPPING OF FURNITURE :

- Place heavier items such as televisions on low-slung furniture.
- Position heavier items far back toward the wall.
- Secure tall pieces of furniture such as bookshelves with braces and anchors.
- Place safety latches or locks on lower drawers to prevent children from opening them.
- Avoid placing toys or desirable objects in places that a child can see but not reach.

◀ Secure bottom drawers of furniture to prevent children from using them as a means to climb. Furniture can easily tip over and injure or kill a child.

Corner and Edge Bumpers

Protect infants and young children from injury on furniture by placing plastic or padded bumpers over sharp edges and corners. Bumpers are designed to prevent injuries or soften falls when children come into contact with furniture. Make sure that corner and edge protectors stay on securely when affixed to furniture edges.

▶ Anchor bookshelves to the wall to prevent them from toppling over.

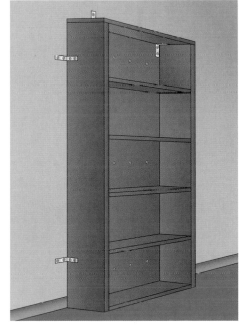

Bunk Beds

Bunk beds are readily available due to their popularity as a child's first "real" bed and the space-saving benefit they offer multichildren families. Although the most common injuries children sustain from bunk beds are due to falls, the U.S. Consumer Product Safety Commission warns of serious injury or even death from strangulation or suffocation when children become trapped between the guardrails and bed frame. The CPSC recommends following these guidelines when purchasing and maintaining a bunk bed in the home:

When purchasing a bunk bed, look for:

■ Side guardrails that are firmly attached to the frame of the bed.

■ Space between bottom guard rail and bed frame no larger than 3½ inches.

■ Guardrails at least 5 inches taller than the mattress surface.

■ Secured weight-bearing cross ties beneath the mattress foundation to prevent the top mattress from shifting or falling.

■ A stable ladder fixed to the frame.

▼ There should be no more than 3½ inches between bunk bed frame boards.

- A mattress designed to fit the bed.

Bunk Bed Maintenance:

- Use 2 secured guardrails on the upper bunk.

- Children under 6 years of age should not sleep in the upper bunk.

- Regularly inspect cross ties to ensure that they are secure under the mattress foundation.

- Teach children not to play on or around bunk beds and to use the ladder, not other furniture, to reach the top bunk.

▼ Adult beds are not designed for infants. A baby can become trapped between the bed and the wall, or the bed and an adjacent piece of furniture. Babies should never sleep with adults because of the risk of suffocation.

Adult Beds

A baby should never be placed on an adult's bed. An infant can become trapped between the bed and the wall or between the bed and the head or footboard. Suffocation or strangulation could be the result. Falls from adult beds often result in injury. The soft bedding used on adult beds is also a suffocation hazard. Even in the presence of a caregiver, babies should not be placed on adult beds. An infant was recently suffocated by an adult who fell asleep while the infant napped. A crib that meets all current safety standards is the best place for your baby to sleep, nap, or wait for a caregiver's full attention.

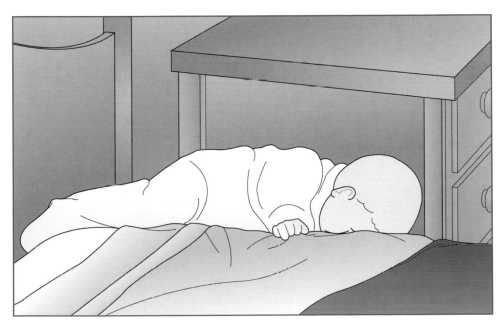

Toy Chests, Trunks, Cedar Chests, Storage Containers

Parents and caregivers should be vigilant with regard to lidded containers found in the home. Storage containers have the potential to injure a child if the lid slams down on the child's head, neck, or limbs, or suffocate the child if she becomes trapped inside. Latched containers that automatically lock and cannot be opened when the lid is pushed from inside should never be used in homes with small children. Children often climb into small spaces to hide or sleep and can suffocate if the container is airtight.

Use the following guidelines with regard to storage containers:

■ Lids on containers should contain supports that prevent the lid from slamming shut.

■ Never use latched containers that automatically lock.

■ Purchase storage containers that have ventilation holes.

■ Remove freely falling lids from toy chests or trunks.

▲ Make sure your child's toy chest contains a support that prevents the lid from falling closed and locking—or remove the lid altogether.

STAIRWAYS

Stairways should be free of clutter and permit unrestricted passage. Avoid placing throw rugs at the bottom of the stairs where they might cause children to slip. Teach your children not to jump from or skip stairs, but to ascend and descend with care using the handrail.

Safety Gates

Very small children and toddlers should be protected from the risk of falls from stairs by the use of safety gates. Safety gates are attached to the wall at the top and bottom of the stairs, preventing access to the stairs themselves. They can also be used to close off any area from which you want to restrict young children. Make sure the gate is securely attached and that your child cannot open it. Look for gates constructed of mesh screen or with openings too small for a child's head. Accordion-style gates manufactured prior to 1985 should be replaced, according to the CPSC, which cites accordion-style gates as an "entrapment hazard."

▼ An infant's head can become lodged in the diamond-shaped spaces of an accordion-style gate. Such gates should be replaced.

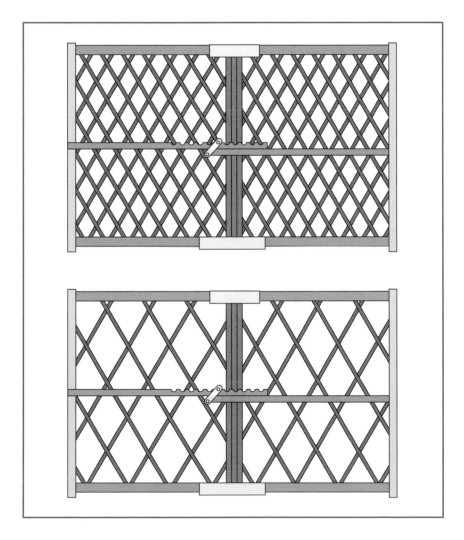

Drowning Hazards

Many things designed to make our lives easier and more relaxing can increase the risk of injury or death to a child. Pools, household buckets, toilets, hot tubs, fish tanks, and of course sinks and bathtubs are all potential drowning hazards, even when holding only small amounts of water. Infants, toddlers, and young children should NEVER be left unattended—or in the care of siblings or other children—around water.

▶ **Many items commonly found in the home are potential drowning hazards for children.**

In surprisingly small quantities, water can be a drowning hazard to children in and around the home.

PREVENT IN-HOME DROWNING DEATHS

- Never leave a baby or small child unattended in the bathtub.

- Bath seats and bath rings are not reliable as safety devices. Do not leave your baby in a bath seat alone in the tub.

- Do not rely on siblings or other children to watch one another in the bath.

- Use a safety latch on the toilet to keep the lid securely closed.

- Keep children away from buckets and pails, even those filled with only small amounts of liquid.

- Secure hot tubs with child proof covers.

- Enclose your pool with a 4-sided fence that contains a self-closing, self-latching gate.

- Empty kiddie pools immediately after adult-supervised use.

- Remove the ladders from above-ground pools when not in use and cover the pool securely.

Tap Water Scalds

The majority of victims of scalding from excessively hot tap water are children under the age of 5 and seniors. Scalds from hot-water taps are serious accidents that often result in injury, even death. Since children often inadvertently burn themselves by failing to properly mix the hot and cold water from the taps, it is best to set the water temperature to a comfortable level. Setting the thermostat of your water heater to 120 degrees F maximum can prevent scalding accidents and save money on heating bills too.

Another option is to install an anti-scald device on showerheads and faucets to regulate the temperature and help prevent burns. These are particularly helpful in apartments or condominiums where inhabitants cannot control the temperature gauge of the water heater.

▶ Water temperature should be set no higher than 120 degrees F.

OVEN

It may be tempting to allow children to play on the kitchen floor while you prepare meals, but it is a dangerous practice. A pan of boiling food or water could drop unexpectedly, putting your child at the risk of a serious burn. The best practice is to have another adult supervise your children when meal preparation demands your attention.

Always store electrical appliances out of a child's reach. Dangling electric cords are irresistible playthings to young children and when pulled may cause the appliance to fall, resulting in injury. Small appliances should be stored away immediately after use.

Turn the handles on pots and pans inward while cooking so they do not extend over the edge of the cooktop. Young children are naturally curious and may reach up and pull the container and its contents down on themselves.

▲ Turn pot handles inward so they are out of reach.

HOUSEHOLD CLEANING PRODUCTS

Cleaning products, pesticides and other poisonous substances are often stored in kitchen cabinets, usually under the kitchen sink. To prevent poisoning, install safety latches or locks on any cabinets in which household products are stored. All household chemicals, even the most innocuous soaps and detergents, should be under lock and key. Purchase safety latches that are easy for you to install and use but impenetrable to children. Child-resistant packaging provides no guarantee; products claiming to have child-resistant enclosures should also be locked away. (See section entitled "Poisons and Other Toxins" for more information.)

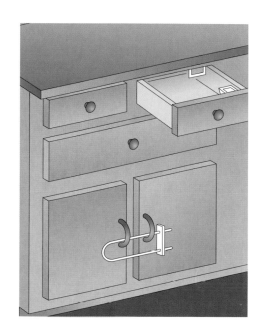

▶ Safety latches are the best method of preventing accidental poisonings.

Hazardous Objects

TOYS

The idea behind a toy is to provide a child with entertainment, education, fun, or some combination of the three, but the actuality is that toys are often the cause of injury. Parents and caregivers must be as vigilant when selecting toys as they are when protecting children from more obvious hazards.

MINIMUM REQUIREMENTS FOR TOYS AND PLAY

- Choose age-appropriate toys.
- Insist that children use toys properly, and supervise young children at play.
- Inspect toys before purchase for quality, design, and construction; inspect toys periodically for breakage, sharp edges, or other hazards.
- Purchase only toys that come with labels and directions.
- Check the U.S. Consumer Product Safety Commission Web site (www.cpsc.gov) for information regarding the recall of toys deemed dangerous or unsuitable.

▲ Regularly examine your child's toys for sharp edges or small pieces that could fit in your child's mouth.

Children under the age of 3 are at greatest risk of toy injury, due, in part, to their propensity for placing small objects in their mouths. Toys and parts of toys should always be larger than a child's mouth. According to the National Safe Kids Campaign, 54 percent of toy-related deaths in 2002 were due to choking, 43 percent of which involved balloons. Since latex balloons are primarily the culprit, Mylar balloons are recommended. Do not allow children to inflate latex balloons; if latex balloons are used, deflate and discard them after use. Toys that make loud or shrill noises should be avoided.

Be wary of cap guns, toy caps, or any toys bearing a label warning that it produces a loud noise. Make sure any electric toy that you purchase is "UL Approved," indicating that the toy has undergone testing by the Underwriters Laboratories.

Toys in the crib are not recommended. The risk of suffocation is greater if there are toys present in the crib. Toys with strings or wires should never be used in or around the crib.

If there is any doubt regarding the safety of a toy, discard it immediately.

GUNS IN THE HOME

If you are a hunter or keep a gun for home protection, there is a very real danger that a firearm may pose a hazard to others, particularly small children who do not know how to handle guns. When storing a gun, your priority as a parent and homeowner should be the safety of your children and of any children or visitors in your home. When firearms are present in the home, family members should be instructed in gun safety.

Along with removing ammunition from all guns AND continuing to treat all firearms as if they were loaded, the following rules should be strictly administered:

- Guns in the home should always be locked in a cabinet.

- Never hide the cabinet key close to the guns where it can be easily discovered; avoid storing the gun-cabinet key with household keys.

- Equip each gun with a trigger lock as extra protection against unauthorized use.

- Store ammunition separately from firearms and under lock and key.

- Always handle a gun as if it were loaded; never point a firearm at anything you do not intend to shoot.

- Don't teach children gun safety yourself. Find a state-approved firearm-safety program to train family members in safe gun-handling practices.

▼ **Guns in homes where children are present are a risk.**

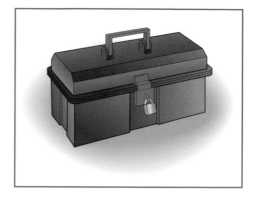

▲ **Keep tools under lock and key.**

TOOLS

The right tools enable you to tackle household projects quickly and correctly, but they must be used and stored with care. Neither hand tools nor power tools should be left unattended or out in the open. Lock tools away in a toolbox or behind the locked doors of a shop. Teach children from a young age that tools are serious business and not intended as playthings. Nor should children be permitted to work with tools without adult supervision. Blades on saws and utility knives should be covered with plastic guards. Chisels usually come in wooden boxes and are best stored in them to protect the tools from rust.

Power tools should be kept behind locked doors with extension cords and power cords disconnected. Remove drill bits and blades from tools when not in use. Never remove safety features such as trigger locks or blade guards from power tools. As an extra safety precaution, add a separate control panel with a master switch in your workshop; that way you can turn off power to all shop outlets with one switch. Keep children and others out of the shop while you are operating power tools.

Movements and conversation by others can distract the tool operator.

According to the *New York Times,* more than 10,000 children 15 years and younger are injured every year by lawnmowers. Children under the age of 12 should not be allowed to operate lawnmowers, and children under 14 should not run a riding lawnmower.

Environmental Influences

ENVIRONMENTAL TOBACCO SMOKE (ETS)

The smoke from a burning cigarette, pipe, or cigar or exhaled from a smoker is known as ETS or secondhand smoke and contains more than 40 compounds known to cause cancer in human beings. The infants and children of parents and caregivers who smoke in the home or around them are particularly vulnerable to secondhand smoke. Not only is there an increased risk of developing cancer, but children exposed to ETS are more likely to develop lower respiratory tract infection and irritation. An increased tendency toward a buildup of fluid in the middle ear—which can lead to ear infections—and slightly reduced lung function are also possible.

Asthma sufferers are particularly sensitive to ETS and experience an increased number of asthma-related episodes as well as an increase in the severity of symptoms. Children without asthma may be more likely to develop the disease if exposed to second handsmoke.

Secondhand smoke is harmful to children.

DON'T GAMBLE WITH YOUR CHILD'S HEALTH— REDUCE EXPOSURE TO ETS

- Make your home a non-smoking environment.

- Don't allow babysitters, caregivers, or people who work in your home to expose your children to secondhand smoke.

- If you must smoke, do so out of doors.

▲ Environmental tobacco smoke is a health hazard.

LEAD

Lead—a toxic substance found in varying quantities in paint, dust, soil, water, food, ceramics, and cosmetics—can adversely affect the health of those exposed to it, with children being particularly vulnerable.

Of greatest concern should be the paint used on houses and apartments built before 1978. According to the U.S. Department of Housing and Urban Development, about 38 million American homes contain some lead paint, and of those homes HUD believes 24 million contain deteriorating lead paint or lead-contaminated dust. If you live in an older house or apartment, have the space checked for lead contamination.

The greatest danger to children is lead paint dust. Lead paint deteriorates, chips, and is ground into dust. Because children play on or around the floor where lead dust settles, it is picked up on the child's hand and transferred from hand to mouth. It can also be breathed into the lungs. Exterior lead paint can contaminate bare soil around the house and endanger children at play.

Paint is not the sole concern when it comes to lead

contamination. Lead pipes, copper pipes with lead solder, and
brass faucets may all contribute
to increased levels of lead in
drinking water. Have the lead
content in your drinking water
tested, particularly if the formula
you feed your baby is made with
tap water. Use bottled water in
the meantime.

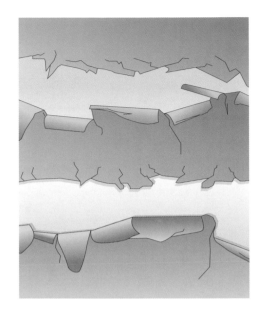

▶ **Peeling lead paint is a serious
health issue for children. Small chips
can be ingested by mouth and the
dust breathed into the lungs.**

PROTECT YOUR CHILDREN FROM LEAD POISONING

- Houses or apartments built
  before 1978 should be tested
  for lead contamination.

- Paint in homes built prior to
  1978 should be well maintained; paint over older surfaces
  with non-lead paint.

- Keep your home free of dust.
  Frequent vacuuming and wiping
  down of areas in which lead
  paint use is suspected can help
  protect children from exposure.

- Replace old, deteriorating windows, doors, or any areas
  where the friction of movement
  causes painted surfaces to rub
  and wear.

- Have your drinking water tested
  for hazardous levels of lead.

- Use bottled water for baby formula.

- Replace older cribs or beds with
  newer models.

- Wash your child's hands frequently.

- Don't allow children to play in
  soil around structures bearing
  deteriorating paint.

- Test floors and walls for lead
  before renovating.

- Consult professionals before renovating areas that contain lead
  paint or lead dust.

**Keeping potentially dangerous products in a locked
cabinet at all times is the best poison prevention.**

POISON HAZARDS

Many chemicals, drugs, cleaning products, pesticides, and cosmetics commonly found in the home pose real poison hazards to young children. Adults can become so accustomed to having convenient access to these products that their potential danger to children is overlooked.

Prescription and over-the-counter drugs, vitamins, mouthwash, detergents, insecticides, cosmetics, and perfume can all be ingested by young children, with disastrous results. Any product that could be toxic when swallowed—or if taken in an overdose—should be stored beyond a child's reach. According to the Consumer Product Safety Commission, nearly a million children under the age of 5 are exposed to medicines and household chemicals every year.

PREVENT CHILD POISONINGS

- Keep all potentially dangerous products in a locked cabinet.

- Never underestimate the curiosity and agility of a child: medicine cabinets and high shelves can be reached and are not necessarily considered safe as storage.

- Insist on child-resistant caps when having prescriptions filled, and make sure containers are tightly closed after each use.

- Do not remove labels from products or transfer contents to other containers.

- Never store food near cleaning products; household cleaning products should be stored separately in their own locked cabinet.

- Avoid opening locks in front of children—curious children are quick to learn.

- Return products to secured storage immediately after use; never leave medications or household products unattended.

- Discard medications that are past their expiration date.

- Never try to deceive your child about medicines or refer to them as "candy."

- Follow directions when using all products, particularly household pesticides.

- Use non-chemical means to control pests.

- Never use insect baits where small children are present.

- Post emergency telephone numbers such as those for the local poison control center, your physician, and the nearest hospital.

HANDLE WITH CARE: EVERYDAY PRODUCTS OF PARTICULAR RISK

- Iron pills; food supplements with iron
- Aspirin and cough medicines
- Insect sprays and baits
- Lighter fluid, kerosene, and charcoal lighter
- Antifreeze
- Furniture polish, turpentine, and solvents

- Products containing lye and acids
- Mouthwashes containing alcohol
- Mothballs and crystals
- Hair spray, cologne, and nail-care products
- Vanilla and almond extracts
- Any brightly colored pills or fluids not meant for consumption

HOUSEPLANTS

Although beautiful, houseplants can be toxic if ingested and may not be suitable in homes with children. Check on the toxicity of a plant before bringing it into your home.

One million children under 5 are exposed to medicines and chemicals every year.

2

Fire

Prevention

Fire Safety Facts

Although 2,670 people were killed in home fires in the United States in 2002 and 389,000 home fires were reported, the good news is that death from fire has dropped 54 percent since 1977 and the number of reported fires has dropped by 46 percent. The National Fire Protection Association cites smoking as the leading cause of home fires that result in death overall, and cooking as the leading cause of home fires and home fire injuries. During the months of December, January, and February, heating equipment accounted for as many deaths by

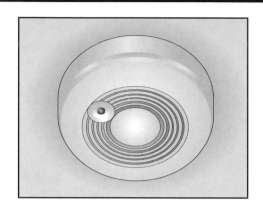

▲ **Smoke detectors save lives!**

fire as did smoking in those same months. The most vulnerable to injury and death are children under 5 and adults over 65, particularly adults 85 and older. Fires cost the nation $5.9 billion in property loss in the year 2002.

How Fires Start and How to Prevent Them

SMOKING

Smoking is the leading cause of fire-related deaths in the United States. Evidence suggests that most of the fires that result in death were caused by smoking materials, such as cigarettes, cigars, or pipes, igniting in bed. If the mounting evidence of the danger of secondhand smoke is not enough to send smokers out-of-doors (if not to the drugstore for a nicotine patch), at minimum smokers should adhere to the following:

Never smoke in bed or if you are sleepy, intoxicated, or taking medication.

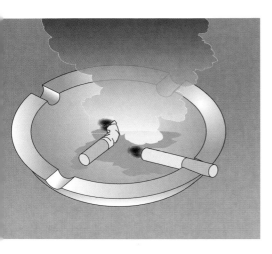

▲ **A burning cigarette left unattended is a fire hazard.**

Keep lit cigarettes, cigars, and pipes, as well as matches and lighters, away from anything combustible such as bedding, mattresses, furniture, curtains, and the like.

Never leave a lit cigarette, cigar, or pipe burning in an ashtray.

Use large, heavy, nontip ashtrays, and never balance ashtrays on armrests or any flammable fabric or furniture.

Soak cigarette butts and cigar ends in water before discarding in the trash.

Before leaving home or going to bed, check under couch and chair cushions for smoldering butts.

Don't leave matches or cigarette lighters lying about, especially if there are children in the house. Keep all fire and smoking materials in a locked cabinet.

Mattresses made after the 1973 Federal Mattress Flammability Standard are safer than earlier models. Replace mattresses manufactured before 1973.

KITCHENS

The leading cause of home fires and home fire injuries is careless cooking. Most kitchen fires start because cooking food has been left unattended. Food, grease, wall coverings, curtains, cabinets, and paper or plastic bags are commonly found in or around a cooking heat source and can easily ignite. Cooking food on the stovetop should NEVER be left unattended.

▲ **Never leave cooking food unattended.**

COOKING SAFELY

- Never leave items cooking on a stovetop unattended.

- Food cooking inside an oven should be closely monitored.

- Keep stovetops, oven doors, and the area around the oven free of towels, potholders, curtains, food packaging, wooden or plastic utensils, or any combustible materials.

- Don't store items over or behind the stove. Boxes of spices are flammable and may cause you to reach across the heated stovetop.

- Wear short or tight-fitting sleeves when cooking to prevent clothing from igniting.

- Children and pets should be kept at least 3 feet away from the stove.

- Fire-retardant potholders and oven mitts should be easily accessible.

- Be vigilant when deep-fat frying. Heat oil slowly, have the lid to the pan close by, and never leave oil unattended.

- Consult your local fire department for information on what type of fire extinguisher to buy and how best to use it.

▶ Keep at least 3 feet of clear space between a portable heater and any other objects, including walls.

HOME HEATING EQUIPMENT

The incidence of home fires due to heating equipment dramatically increases during the months of December, January, and February. More than one eighth of these annual fires are caused by space-heating equipment according to the U.S. Fire Administration. Portable electric or kerosene heaters, wood-burning stoves, fireplaces with inserts, and room gas heaters are commonly involved in home heating fires, particularly when equipment is poorly maintained or misused.

Portable Electric or Kerosene Heaters

Electric or liquid fuel (kerosene) heaters must be at least 3 feet away from any combustible material such as furniture, bedding, clothing, or window coverings. Never leave portable

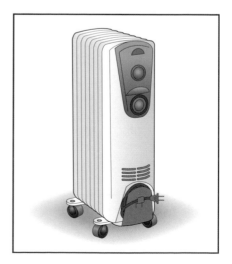

▶ Protect yourself from burns when you cook by wearing oven mitts and a shirt with tight-fitting sleeves.

heaters in operation when you leave the room or go to sleep. Children and pets should not be left alone with a running heater.

When purchasing an electric heater, look for the Underwriters Laboratories (UL) safety certification. Electric heaters should also be equipped with a safety switch that automatically turns off the unit if the heater turns over. Electric heaters should be checked frequently for frayed or damaged wires.

Kerosene heaters should be used only in well-ventilated rooms and like electric heaters should come with a UL listing. Turn the heater off and allow it to cool prior to refueling, and take care not to overfill. Use the

WHAT TO DO IF A GREASE FIRE STARTS

- Using an oven mitt or potholder, place a lid over the burning pan.
- Turn off the heat source.
- Leave the lid on the pan until it is completely cool.
- Never use water on a grease fire.
- Don't attempt to carry a pan on fire to the sink. Smother the fire with a lid and leave the pan where it is.

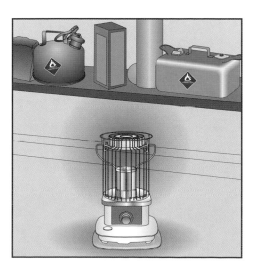

fuel recommended by the unit's manufacturer. Never substitute a different type of fuel. Kerosene should be stored separately from the heating unit in an approved container that is clearly marked. Some communities forbid the use of kerosene heaters, so check on the legality of use in your area.

◀ Store fuel far from the heating unit.

Fireplaces

A fire burning in the fireplace is a simple pleasure and with a little care and maintenance can be a delight from year to year. It's a good idea to have the chimney inspected at the start of the fall season for any buildup of creosote, a substance that—if allowed to accumulate—can cause chimney fires. A certified specialist will also check for any obstructions or cracks within the chimney.

To ensure safe operation when burning a fire, always use a fireplace screen that covers the entire opening. Never burn debris, paper, or wood from an unknown source. Use only seasoned hardwoods specifically sold for use in fireplaces, or artificial logs manufactured for use in fireplaces. Build fires toward the back of the fireplace or on a grate designed for use within a fireplace.

Extinguish fires before retiring for the night or before leaving the home.

Wood Stoves

Proper installation and regular maintenance are key to the safety of wood-burning stoves. The wood stove you purchase should be certified by a recognized testing laboratory and constructed of plate steel or cast-iron. Follow the manufacturer's recommendations when installing. The surface beneath a wood stove should be noncombustible or the stove should be placed on a code-specified floor protector. The chimney connection and flue on a wood stove should be inspected for creosote buildup at the onset of the heating season by a specialist. Never use gasoline or other flammable liquids to start a fire, nor should you burn artificial logs in a wood stove.

▼ The Underwriters Laboratories symbol indicates that a product has been tested for compliance with regard to safe public use.

Clothes Dryers

While most home appliances are used without incident, the U.S. Consumer Product Safety Commission estimates that 15,500 fires associated with clothes dryers take place annually. The lack of dryer maintenance, the buildup of lint, inadequate venting, or placing of inappropriate items in the dryer are cited as contributing factors. Follow these simple safety measures to reduce the chance of a fire:

- Clean lint filters before and after each cycle, and never operate a dryer without a filter.

- Never leave a dryer operating if you are not home.

- Dryers should be ventilated to the exterior, not a wall, basement, or attic.

- Installation and periodic maintenance should be done by a professional.

- Don't place items containing foam or other combustible materials—such as rugs and athletic shoes—in the dryer.

- Use the appropriate electrical outlet for dryers and all major appliances.

- Never store combustibles such as boxes, newspaper, clothing, and other similar items on or around the dryer

CEILING LIGHT FIXTURES

A burning incandescent lightbulb can generate a great deal of heat. An exposed bulb perpendicular to the ceiling dissipates heat into the surrounding air, but a bulb in a light fixture flush against the ceiling lacks this protective air barrier and can overheat. To prevent overheating and possible ignition, flush-mounted ceiling light fixtures should be insulated.

Never install a bulb with a higher wattage than the fixture is designed to hold. Bulbs of higher wattage can overheat the socket wiring and start a fire. Look for the recommended watt rating stamped somewhere on the fixture and heed the limit.

HALOGEN LIGHTING

Halogen bulbs burn at a hotter temperature than incandescent bulbs. Flammable material that comes into contact with a halogen bulb can easily ignite. Halogen bulbs are also frequently used in standing floor lamps, which if overturned can put the bulb in contact with combustible material or cause the bulb to explode and ignite. The Consumer Product Safety Commission offers the following safety tips when purchasing or using lamps containing halogen bulbs:

- Make sure the lamp features a protective wire guard that shields the bulb from coming into contact with flammable materials.

- Never place the lamp near draperies, clothing, or bedding.

- Turn the lamp off when you leave the room.

- Halogen lamps are not advised where children and pets are about.

- Use a halogen bulb of 300 watts or less.

COMBUSTIBLE MATERIAL

Combustible materials are any substances that readily ignite and burn such as gasoline, paint solvents and strippers, turpentine, oil, and similar substances. These materials pose the risk of fire as well as the ill effects from breathing in their fumes. Read and follow all container warnings for combustible materials. Never use or store combustible materials near open flames or appliance pilot lights. Use latex or water-based paint products rather than alkyd (oil-based) products when possible. Always store paint or combustible products in their original containers, and be sure containers are equipped with tight-fitting lids.

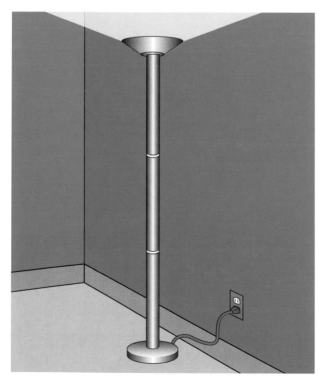

◀ Standing halogen lamps can easily tip over and should be equipped with a wire shield.

Gasoline

Gasoline is a highly flammable and potentially explosive material and should be handled with great care. If you must store gasoline to fuel garden, lawn, or other equipment, observe the following guidelines:

■ Buy small quantities of gasoline and store it in a UL-approved container in a shed or detached garage, never in the house.

■ Never use gasoline to start a fire in a fireplace, wood stove, or charcoal grill.

■ Do not use gasoline as a solvent for cleaning tools or machine parts.

■ Never use gasoline near a heater, furnace, or appliance pilot light. Gasoline fumes are heavier than air and settle near the floor, where they can be ignited by a pilot light.

■ Allow lawn equipment to cool before refueling it.

■ Never leave gasoline within reach of children.

HAZARDOUS WASTE

Hazardous waste such as motor oil, fuel additives, adhesives and glues, fuels, pesticides and insecticides, oil-based paints, solvents, stains, and finishes should be

▲ Store combustible materials such as gasoline in approved canisters.

recycled or taken to hazardous-waste disposal sites. Call your local environmental, health, or solid-waste agency for instructions on how best to dispose of home hazardous waste or visit the U.S. Environmental Protection Agency Web site at www.epa.gov.

HOLIDAY DECORATIONS

Candles

While the statistics cited earlier in this chapter reflect good news about the decrease in the number of home fires in general, fires started by candles have tripled in the last decade. Holidays, particularly Christmas and New Year's Day, represent peak days of fires reported.

CANDLE SAFETY

- Never leave a lit candle unattended, even for a moment.

- Remove all flammable items from the area in which you plan to burn a candle, including decorations, curtains, paper, plants, and fabrics.

- Candleholders should be large, heavy, and difficult to tip over.

- Place candles on a flat, sturdy, uncluttered surface.

- Never put candles on a windowsill or near hanging window treatments.

- Flammable liquids should never be stored near a lit candle.

- Be sure all candles are extinguished before going to sleep.

- Candles, matches, and lighters should be kept in a locked cabinet when adults are not present.

Christmas Trees

According to the National Safety Council, more than 400 residential fires a year involve Christmas trees; the National Fire Protection Association cites lights, cords, and plugs as the most common sources of ignition. An artificial tree is a safer option than a live tree since many new models are fire-resistant. (Check for a label stating that the artificial tree you are purchasing is fire-resistant.) If you purchase and display a live tree observe the following safety tips:

- Buy a fresh, green tree. Needles should be flexible and should not fall easily from the branches.

- Cut off an extra 2 inches from the tree trunk so the tree can absorb water.

- Place the tree in a sturdy stand that holds at least a quart of water and check the water level frequently.

- Position the tree away from any heat sources such as a fireplace, space heater, baseboard heat, or electronic appliance.

- Use only electric lights that have been tested and UL approved; such lights will be labeled accordingly.

- If you are decorating the tree indoors, use lights manufactured for indoor use.

- Check tree lights to be sure wire insulation is intact and sockets and bulbs are in good shape. Replace any frayed or broken lights.

- No more than 3 sets of lights should be used per extension cord.

- Lit candles should never be used as tree decorations, and electric lights should not be used on metal trees.

- Never leave a lit tree unattended. Turn off the tree lights when leaving the room or going to sleep.

- A dry tree is a fire hazard. Dispose of the tree as soon as it begins dropping needles, and don't leave the tree in the house or garage after it has been taken down.

▲ **Make sure your live Christmas tree has plenty of water.**

Fire Detection and Prevention Devices

SMOKE DETECTORS

There is a reason federal law requires smoke detectors be installed in public access buildings: SMOKE ALARMS SAVE LIVES! Smoke detectors have reduced death by home fires by at least half since the 1970s, when they were introduced, according to the National Fire Protection Association. Although 95 percent of the homes in the United States are equipped with at least one smoke detector, in 25 percent of the homes in which fires were reported—and in which there were smoke detectors— the detectors did not work. The presence of smoke alarms is not enough; the devices must be tested frequently and the batteries changed every year.

> The single most important preventive measure you can take is to equip your home with working smoke detectors.

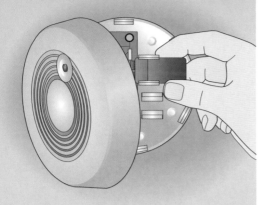

◄ Check batteries once a month and change them once a year.

▼ Smoke detectors save lives by providing an early warning of fire.

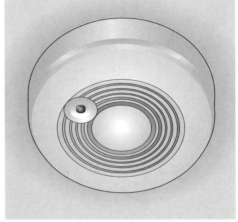

SMOKE DETECTOR PLACEMENT AND MAINTENANCE

- Every level of the home should be equipped with at least one smoke alarm.

- Install an additional alarm outside each sleeping area.

- Test detectors every month.

- Replace batteries annually.

- Replace batteries when you change your clocks in order to remember.

- Familiarize all family members with the sound of the alarm.

- Smoke rises. Install alarms on the ceiling or high on the wall.

- Avoid placing alarms near windows, exterior doors, or anywhere a draft may interfere with their effectiveness.

- Don't paint smoke detectors.

- Replace smoke detectors every ten years.

- Smoke alarms with strobe lights are available for the hearing impaired.

FIRE EXTINGUISHERS

The number-one priority during a fire should be getting everyone out of the home safely. A fire extinguisher can be used to arrest small fires and to limit the spread of fire until the fire department arrives, but the presence of a fire extinguisher does not mean that you should handle any fire or try to do the work of professional firefighters.

Installing a fire extinguisher in your kitchen, garage, basement, or furnace area may help to stop a small fire if you are present at the moment of ignition. Know how to use each fire extinguisher in your home.

BE EXTINGUISHER SAVVY

- Know what you're buying: grease fires are different from electrical fires. Consult your local fire department for the most effective extinguisher for the area it will be stored in.

- Learn how to use the device before a fire occurs. Read all instructions and labels.

- Install extinguishers in the kitchen, garage, basement, and anywhere fire is likely to occur.

- Position fire extinguishers near an exit so that you can safely leave the area if the fire becomes overwhelming.

- Know when to exit. Large fires should be abandoned immediately and the fire department summoned.

▲ It is important that you know how to use the fire extinguishers in your home.

HOME SPRINKLER SYSTEMS

Automatic fire sprinkler systems are designed to react quickly: a thermostat registers elevated temperature in the room and a sprinkler head is activated. Because of their quick response, sprinkler systems reduce the amount of heat, smoke, and fire and can save lives. The National Fire Protection Association (NFPA) states that chance of death by fire and property loss are reduced one-half to two-thirds when sprinklers are present. Newly constructed homes can be equipped with home sprinkler systems, and the NFPA recommends their installation. Sprinklers can also be installed as a retrofit to protect existing housing. Homeowners' insurance premiums may be reduced by the addition of a home sprinkler system.

According to the Home Fire Sprinkler Coalition, home sprinklers use much less water than fire department hoses and add only 1.5 percent to the cost of a new construction. Accidental discharges are quite rare.

Maintenance and regular inspection by a professional are required. Never paint any part of the sprinkler system and be sure to include working smoke detectors even if your home is equipped with a sprinkler system.

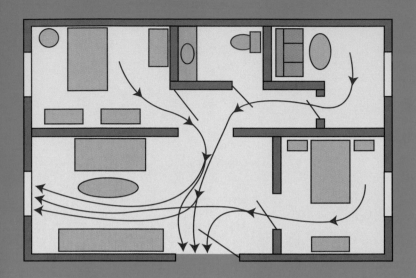

◄ **Everyone in the family should know the emergency exit plan.**

EXIT PLAN

Although it's frightening to think about a fire in your home, taking the time to establish an exit plan may save your life and the lives of those you love. Time is of the essence and an escape plan that is well rehearsed will become second nature. Don't wait until an emergency occurs to figure out how to best handle it. Every member of the family should know the exit plan and be well practiced in it.

PLANNING FOR A FIRE CAN SAVE LIVES!

■ Figure out two ways out of each room; alternative exits may include a window, roof, or safety ladder.

■ Windows secured with bars should be taken into consideration. Quick releases should be available on security bars, and all family members should know how to operate them.

■ Test smoke alarms once a month and make sure everyone in the family is familiar with the sound of the alarm.

■ Practice an actual escape plan two times a year and have everyone in the family participate.

■ Hold a fire drill at night once everyone in the family has practiced the escape plan.

■ Agree on a central meeting place.

FIRE RULES EVERYONE SHOULD KNOW

- Before exiting a room in a fire, feel the door to check the temperature. If the door feels normal to the touch, open it partway and check to see that the hallway is free of fire.

- Crawl low in a fire or smoke-filled room and keep mouth covered.

- If a door is hot to the touch, do not open it. Turn to an alternate escape route, usually a window.

- "Stop, Drop, and Roll" is the rule. If clothes catch fire, stop, drop to the floor or ground, and roll repeatedly to put out the fire.

- Escape the fire, then call the fire department.

- Never go back into a burning building.

Remember that the single most important preventive measure you can take is to install working smoke detectors on every level of the home. Make sure each detector is equipped with fresh batteries and that the batteries are never borrowed for use elsewhere. Getting all family members out of the building should be the number-one priority if a fire occurs. While the immediate impulse may be to fight the fire, the safest course is to get every one out and to summon the fire department immediately.

3

Electricity

and
Heating

Electricity Basics

ELECTRIC SERVICE ENTRANCE PANEL

Every adult residing in a home or apartment should know where the service entrance panel is located and how to turn off the power should the need arise. Electricity enters the home and its flow is controlled through the service entrance panel. From the main panel the power wires branch into separate circuits and are routed throughout the house.

An older home may have a main panel with a disconnect switch, a bus bar, and a ground conductor. If so, the panel serves only as a distribution box and a main disconnector. Some older homes may be wired directly to a main panel, without subpanels, in which case each circuit has its own fuse within the main panel. Newer homes are likely to have panels with built-in breakers.

Familiarize yourself with the electric service entrance panel in your home. Identify which type of main shutoff you have and which breakers (or fuses) control each circuit.

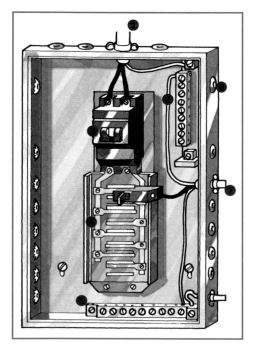

◄ Main components of an electric service entrance panel.
1. Power supply from meter
2. Neutral bus
3. Main disconnector
4. Hot bus
5. Ground bus
6. Knockout
7. Cable to house circuit

ELECTRICAL SAFETY TIPS

- Always turn the power off at the electric service entrance panel when you intend to work on any circuit.

- Do not overload a receptacle with adapters and extension cords.

- Do not run extension cords under carpets or throw rugs.

- When holding electric razors, hair dryers, or any bath or kitchen appliance, do not touch faucets or plumbing pipes, as most electrical systems are grounded through the plumbing system.

- Keep radios, hair dryers, and other electrical appliances a safe distance from the bathtub when bathing.

- When adapting a three-prong plug to a two-prong receptacle, make sure the adapter is grounded to the screw on the receptacle's cover plate and that the box is grounded.

- Never install a substitute fuse with an amperage rating greater than the one you are replacing.

- Never pull a plug from a receptacle by its cord; this puts wear on the plug and could create a fire hazard.

- Always unplug an appliance or lamp before attempting to repair it.

- Before starting any work, always test the power to make sure it is off. Use a voltage tester or a lamp or small appliance.

- Do not use an aluminum ladder when working on overhead service lines or when testing live currents.

- If you must work on wet floors, wear rubber boots and stand on planks to place a buffer between you and the moisture.

- Never touch pipes when working on electrical projects since most electrical systems are grounded to metal plumbing.

- When making plumbing repairs, take care not to splice into a plumbing line that also serves as a grounding conductor.

CIRCUIT BREAKERS AND FUSES

Each circuit is protected by a breaker or fuse. Breakers have replaced fuses for the most part, and renewable, switch-type breakers are typically found on modern panels. Breakers—and fuses before them—are a kind of safety buffer that prevents electrical fires when one of three things has happened: a circuit has been overloaded, a circuit has shorted, or a fuse has become loosened. Any of these will cause the breaker to "trip," disrupting the flow of electricity to the circuit. The breaker simply needs to be turned back on. However if breakers continually trip in the home, it is important to determine and deal with the cause.

RECEPTACLE OUTLET SAFETY

Proper maintenance and use of the electrical receptacles in the home can reduce the chance of electric shock and fire. Damaged, deteriorated, or outdated receptacles should be repaired or upgraded by a licensed electrician.

Ground Fault Circuit Interrupters

To prevent electrical shock from a ground fault, your bathroom, kitchen, laundry room, and

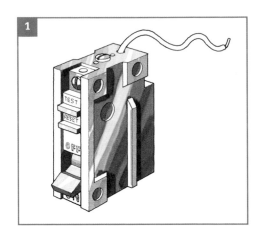

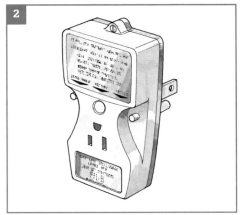

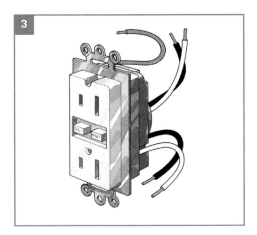

1 GFCI breaker—This protects an entire circuit from inside the panel.
2 GFCI receptacle—This protects the outlet it is in and all outlets after it on a circuit.
3 GFCI adapter—This protects only the receptacle it is plugged into.

workshop receptacles should be equipped with ground fault circuit interrupters, GFCIs. You can get GFCI protection in one of three devices. The most expensive and most versatile GFCI is contained in a breaker (1, facing page). When you install a GFCI breaker, everything on that circuit is protected. The second device is a GFCI receptacle that is easily installed (2). When you install this receptacle, all receptacles on the circuit after the GFCI are also protected. The last alternative is the simplest. It is a GFCI receptacle adapter (3). You simply plug this adapter into a standard receptacle and then plug your appliances into the adapter. An adapter works well but protects only the receptacle it is plugged into.

LIGHTING MAINTENANCE

Replacing a Bulb

Follow these simple steps and precautions to replace a light-bulb safely:

- Dry your hands before working with electricity.

- Turn off the fixture switch and turn off the circuit through the breaker at the electric service entrance panel.

- Check the fixture label for correct wattage of the bulb to avoid overheating. If no watt size is indicated, replace the old bulb with a new one of the same wattage.

- Hold the bulb by the glass end only; never touch the metal base while screwing in the bulb.

Broken bulbs require special handling. Disconnect the lamp and turn off the power to the circuit. Use a pair of needle-nose pliers to twist the bulb loose. If you don't have a pair of pliers handy, press the end of a bar of soap into the broken base, taking care not to cut yourself. Twist the bar of soap slowly to unscrew the bulb base from the socket. When replacing the new bulb, take care not to overtighten; this can increase the chance of breakage.

Replacing a Fixture

To remove an old fixture:

- Turn off the power to the circuit that supplies electricity to the fixture.

- Loosen the set screws or center nut that hold the glass globe or diffuser to the fixture.

- With the diffuser removed, unscrew the center nut or screws from the decorative base.

- Pull the base down to expose the mounting wires and mounting strap.

- Remove the strap from the box and pull the wires out.

- Separate the wire connections and the fixture will come free.

To Replace a New Fixture

- Fasten the mounting strap to the ceiling box.

- If the fixture requires it, turn the threaded nipple into the strap.

- Hold the fixture up to the ceiling box so the fixture's lead wires can be attached to the wires in the box.

- Electrical wires are color-coded; connect each wire in the fixture—black, white, and bare copper or green to the same colored wire in the box (e.g., black to black, white to white, and copper to copper). Do not twist or tape wires together; use only UL-approved wire connectors, known as wire nuts. (No bare wire should be showing.)

- Fasten the base either to the strap with mounting screws or to the threaded nipple with a nut.

- Attach the globe to the fixture.

- Never insert a bulb with a higher wattage rating than the fixture is designed to hold.

Heating Systems

FURNACE MAINTENANCE

For both safety and economy, your furnace and flue should be inspected by a professional service person before each heating season begins. Homeowners can perform the following services to keep both gas- and oil-fired furnaces in good operating condition.

Change furnace filters frequently—at least once per month during peak heating and (if you have central air-conditioning) cooling seasons. Clean filters will help keep the furnace, ducts, and house clean.

Lubricate blower motor bearings in accordance with the manufacturer's service manual.

Vacuum ducts and air registers to keep them free of dust.

Each time you change filters, inspect the vent area for rust or scale and call a service person if either is present.

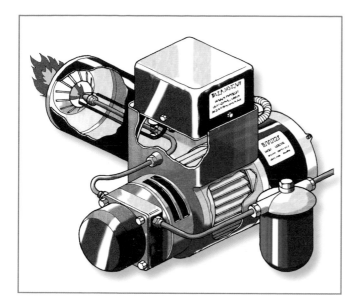

Gas furnaces require less frequent cleaning, maintenance, and adjustment than do oil-fired furnaces. Do-it-yourselfers can clean gas-fired furnaces once every two to three years. A qualified HVAC (heating, ventilation, and air-conditioning) service technician should inspect flame and pilot mechanisms once a year. The main gas supply line, pilot light, and burners should be turned off prior to beginning any task.

Because oil-fired furnaces require a little more complicated technology to operate than do gas furnaces, they need to be serviced more frequently. Most do-it-yourselfers can handle the tasks associated with cleaning a pressure-type oil burner.

Servicing Oil Burners—

1 Change furnace filter: Place a tray beneath work area. Unscrew cup. Remove and replace cartridge and gasket.

2 Lubricate motor: Find oil cups at the ends of motor. Squirt 3–6 drops of 10W nondetergent electric motor oil in each cup. Don't over lubricate.

3 Clean pump strainer: Remove pump cover and gasket. Soak strainer in solvent, then brush clean. Replace with new gasket. (Be advised that some pumps do not have strainers.)

4 Clean fan: Unbolt transformer and swing aside to access fan. Clean blades with bottle brush or lint-free cloth attached to stick. Wipe interior of housing with rag.

Heating System Troubleshooting

The failure of a home heating system is inconvenient, uncomfortable, and could lead to major home repair problems if the failure occurs while residents are away during a winter freeze. The best practice is to have heating systems regularly maintained and inspected by an HVAC professional. If your heating system fails to work, check to see whether one of the more common faults, summarized below, is responsible:

Symptom: Hissing or banging sounds coming from boiler or pipe work.

Cause: A coal furnace may have a blocked chimney. Check for buildup in the flue of soot, and have the chimney swept.

or

Cause: Heavy mineral deposits have built up due to hard water. Turn off the boiler and pump, treat the system with a descaler, then drain, flush, and restart system.

or

Cause: Faulty boiler thermostat. Turn off the boiler but leave the pump running to circulate water and cool the system. When the ststem is cool, try to operate the boiler thermostat control. If there is no clicking sound present, a repairperson is required to fix the thermostat.

or

Cause: Steam systems may have pipe work that is not sloped correctly. Radiators and pipes must run downward so water can travel freely back to the boiler. Check radiators and pipes with a spirit level.

or

Cause: A coal furnace's circulating pump may not be working. Turn off the boiler to see whether the pump is operating. If it is not, turn off the power and check the wires connected to the pump. If the pump runs but the outlet pipe is cool, check for an air lock using a bleed screw. If the pump is still not working, it may be blocked and need to be cleaned or replaced.

Symptom: Water boiler's pressure-relief valve opens, sending water through overflow pipe.

Cause: There may be excess pressure in the pipe caused by a malfunction in the expansion tank. The expansion tank may need to be replaced.

Symptom: Radiators are cold even though boiler is operating.

Cause: Pump may not be working. Check the pump motor for vibration. If the pump is running, check for an air lock by opening the bleed valve. If this has no effect, the pump outlet may be blocked, which means it needs to be cleaned or replaced.

or

Cause: Pump thermostat or timer is set incorrectly or is faulty. Check both thermostat and timer and reset if necessary. If settings are okay, turn off the power and check the wiring connection to the pump. If the connections are in good shape, call in a repairperson.

Symptom: Radiators in one part of house do not warm up.

Cause: Timer or thermostat that controls zone valve is faulty or not set properly. Check the timer or thermostat setting and reset if necessary. If this does not help, turn off the power supply and check wire connections. If this is to no avail, call a repairperson.

or

Cause: Zone valve is faulty. The system will need to be drained and the zone valve replaced.

Symptom: A single radiator does not heat up.

Cause: The manual inlet valve is closed. Check the setting of the valve and open it if necessary.

or

Cause: The thermostatic radiator valve is faulty or not set properly. Check the setting of the valve and reset if necessary. If this has no effect, the valve should be replaced.

or

Cause: The return valve is not set properly. Remove the return valve cover and adjust the valve setting until radiator heats. Have the valve properly balanced during the next service visit.

or

Cause: The inlet or outlet of the radiator is blocked by corrosion. The radiator must be removed, flushed out, or replaced.

Symptom: Top of radiator is cool while bottom is warm.

Cause: An air lock at the top of the radiator is preventing water from circulating. Operate the bleed valve to release the trapped air.

Symptom: Center of radiator is cool while top and ends are warm.

Cause: Heavy deposits of corrosion may be restricting circulation of water. The radiator must be removed and flushed out or replaced.

Symptom: Water leaking from system.

Cause: Pipe unions at joints, pump, or boiler may be loose. Switch off boiler and turn off furnace completely. Turn off pump and tighten leaking joints. If this has no effect, joints may need to be remade completely.

or

Cause: Split or punctured pipes may be present. Damaged pipes can be temporarily wrapped in rags. Switch off the boiler and pump and make temporary repairs with sealant. Pipes will have to be replaced or professionally repaired.

Symptom: Boiler is not working.

Cause: The timer or programmer is malfunctioning. Check to see that the unit is turned on and set correctly. Replace if fault persists.

or

Cause: The pilot light has gone out. Relight a gas-boiler pilot light following the manufacturer's instructions, which are usually found on the back of the boiler's front panel. If the pilot light fails after repeated tries, call a repairperson.

4

Environmental Emergencies

Preparing for an Environmental Emergency

Although it's not much fun to think about the possibility of life-endangering weather, natural disasters, a major chemical emergency, or the effects of contaminants found in our environment, a little foresight and planning could mean the difference between surviving a difficult time and experiencing injury, ill health, or even death.

In the event of a hurricane, flooding, earthquake, or other disaster, city, state, or federal relief workers will most likely be on the scene, but that doesn't mean that help or relief will be imminent. Other priorities may require official attention, leaving some members of the population unattended for hours or even days. The most prudent action is to prepare for an emergency before it occurs.

▲ Everyone in the family should know what to do should an emergency arise.

EMERGENCY PLANNING

The Federal Emergency Management Agency (FEMA) recommends that every household have an emergency plan in place. Establish an emergency plan and discuss it with all the members of the family. Educate yourself about the natural disasters most likely to occur in your area. Organizations such as the American Red Cross can provide information about how best to deal with local emergencies.

Make sure that all members of the family, including children, are aware of the family's emergency plan and what to do should a specific emergency arise. Discuss the types of potential emergencies and how best to deal with them.

Create a floor plan of your home and establish two possible escape routes from each room. Learn how to turn off utilities such as water, gas, and electricity.

Emergency telephone numbers should be easily accessible, and children should know how to contact the police, fire department, and 911. Choose a local point person as well as someone out of state to be the person family members call if they are separated. Establish two locations—one outside the home in the event of a fire, the other in an outlying area if it is impossible to return home during a disaster—where the family will agree to meet. At least one family member should take first aid and CPR instruction. Put together an emergency supplies kit.

EMERGENCY SUPPLIES KIT

When disaster strikes you may not have the time or opportunity to purchase supplies. FEMA recommends that you prepare an emergency supplies kit by buying and storing items necessary for survival and comfort if basic services—electricity, gas, water, and telephones—are cut off. The emergency supplies kit is an important part of the emergency planning that everyone should do. FEMA suggests not only that every home contain an emergency supplies kit but that you also outfit your car with a smaller version of the kit. (Your car kit should also contain booster cables, a fire extinguisher, a shovel, and a tire repair kit and pump.) FEMA also recommends that your home be equipped with a portable container such as a backpack, duffel bag, or cargo container in which to carry emergency supplies should you need to evacuate the home.

EMERGENCY SUPPLIES KIT

■ FEMA recommends that an emergency supplies kit contain the following:

■ Battery-powered radio or television and extra batteries

■ Flashlight and extra batteries

■ First-aid kit and manual

■ Prescription medicines if needed

■ Cash and a credit card

■ Picture identification

■ Extra set of car keys

■ Matches in a waterproof container

■ Signal flare

■ Maps of the area

■ Emergency phone numbers

■ Special needs such as diapers, formula, hearing-aid batteries, wheelchair battery, extra pair of eyeglasses

FEMA also suggests that emergency supplies of water, food, and other essentials for living be stored in the home, ready for use or evacuation:

■ Three gallons of water per person

■ A three-day to one-week supply of nonperishable food

■ A wrench to turn off utilities

■ A manual can opener and utility knife

■ Heavy-duty garbage bags and bucket with a tight-fitting lid (for makeshift toilet)

■ Blankets and sleeping bags for each family member

■ Household liquid bleach (to treat drinking water)

■ Sanitation and hygiene items such as toilet paper, premoistened towelettes, and sanitary napkins and tampons.

WATER

FEMA recommends that a three-day supply of fresh drinking water be stored in plastic containers with tightly fitting lids. Milk cartons or glass bottles can decompose or break and are not recommended. You should have a minimum of three gallons per person, more if possible, stored in an accessible place. Don't count on there being time to fill empty containers with tap water in the event of a disaster or emergency.

Potable water will also be available in the water heater, in the toilet tank (if not disinfected), in the water pipes, or from melted ice cubes.

WATER PURIFICATION

Boil impure water to ensure safe drinking. If water contains large particles or impurities, strain it through a clean cloth before boiling. Boil water for one full minute, then cool before drinking.

Household liquid bleach will also purify water. For every gallon of water, add 16 drops of bleach. Mix the solution and let stand for 30 minutes. If the water does not smell slightly of chlorine, repeat the procedure and let stand 15 minutes. If the water still lacks the scent of chlorine, throw it away and find another source of water.

Water purification tablets can be purchased from camping goods stores and stored in your emergency supplies kit.

FOOD

Along with water, FEMA suggests that a three-day supply of nonperishable food be available in the home or for evacuation. Foods that don't need refrigeration, cooking, or and use little or no water are best. Canned meats, fruits, vegetables, juices, milk, and soup are all ready to eat and contain large amounts of liquid. Peanut butter, jelly, granola, and candy bars can provide a quick source of protein and/or fat. Consider individually sized canned goods and prepackaged beverages: pull-tops lids and vacuum-packed containers make them easy to open and long lasting. Don't forget to include a supply of specialty food, such as infant formula, canned baby foods, or diet items for those with health problems.

NO ELECTRICITY? HERE'S WHAT TO EAT FIRST!

- First: Perishable food and food from the refrigerator.

- Second: Food from the freezer. (Frozen foods should last 3 days if you minimize the number of times the freezer door is opened.)

- Third: Crackers, cookies, snack foods, and peanut butter.

- Last: Canned goods and non-perishables.

WEATHER RADIOS

The National Weather Service offers continuous broadcasts of weather forecasts, conditions, watches, and warnings, and the broadcasts can be received on the National Oceanic and Atmospheric Administration (NOAA) Weather Radio. All types of hazards, both natural (severe flooding, earthquakes, hurricanes, etc.) and technological (chemical releases or toxic spills) are broadcast, making it a comprehensive source for weather and emergency information. FEMA and the National Weather Service recommend the purchase of a radio with both a battery backup and a specific area message encoder (SAME). The encoder provides you with county-specific information in an emergency, thus giving instantaneous access to watches, warnings, or life-threatening conditions in your area.

Turning Utilities On or Off

It is important to know how to turn on and off your home's utilities should the need arise. The first step is to turn off all standing pilot lights and then to turn off the main shutoff valves of the utilities. Utility providers can educate you as to the valve's location as well as how to turn it off. You can paint or otherwise mark the shutoff valves to make them easy to locate and identify.

To avoid electrical fires or shock in the event of storm damage, turn off the current to all electrical circuits in the electric service entrance panel.

If you reside in a home, turn off the gate valve to the water supply pipe on the street side of the water meter to shut off the water supply. If your water comes from a well, shut off the valve at the top of the well pump or on the supply pipe from the well to the house.

Each family member should know the location of utility shutoff valves.

Experts advise not to shut off the gas during earthquakes; wait until the quake has stopped and turn gas off only if you smell gas.

To prevent a gas fire or explosion, shut off natural gas at the meter. Most shutoff valves require use of a wrench to shut off gas service. To avoid having to search for a wrench during an emergency, purchase one of the correct size and hang it near the shutoff valve. If you do shut off

▼ All family members should know how to turn the electricity off at the electric service entrance panel.

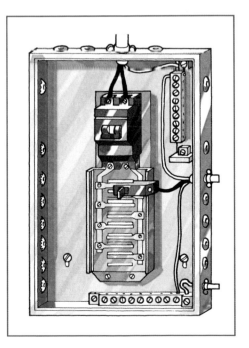

the gas, remember that there may be leaks that have not been repaired. Let a professional serviceperson check that everything is in working order before turning the gas back on.

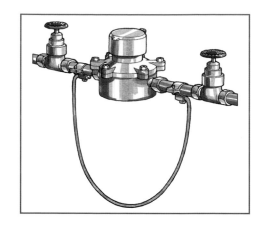

▶ **Water meters are made of brass and are usually about 6 inches in diameter.**

Emergency Backup

GENERATORS

Portable generators—or even permanently installed standby systems—are becoming more popular as backup power systems in the event of power failure. Portable generators of at least 5,000 watts can keep "survival appliances" such as refrigerators, well pumps, lights, and heating systems running, according to an article in the *New York Times* ("Providing Electricity When the Power Fails," June 13, 2004).

Power transfer switches, which connect the generator directly to the main electric panel in the home, do away with the need to plug appliances into the generator. The switches also allow the house to be disconnected from the utility grid, which is impor-

tant for the safety of utility workers, who can be injured or killed by a generator's power backtracking through the grid. Another concern is the carbon monoxide portable generators produce, which makes a safe location out of doors key to their safe operation. Inside basements, garages, and directly outside windows are not safe places to install portable generators.

▼ **Portable generators can provide back up in the event of a power failure.**

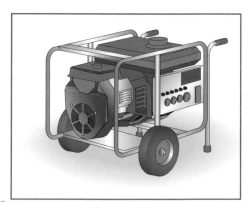

COOKING AND HEATING

If you live in areas of extreme cold, where blizzards are common, you should have a backup heat source such as a fireplace or portable heater for emergency use. A charcoal grill can be used as an emergency cook stove; keep a few bags of charcoal and a can of charcoal lighter fluid handy. Even if you lack a grill, the charcoal can be placed in a pit dug in the ground or in a metal pail and burned for cooking or warmth. Observe normal precautions for open flames and don't burn charcoal indoors without adequate ventilation. A camp stove, propane lantern, or even a candle placed in an aluminum can provides a cooking and heating source.

TOILET

If toilet or other water drains are plugged, do not continue to run water or waste into sinks or toilet bowls. You can use a camp toilet or make one by fitting a heavy-duty plastic trash bag into a plastic or metal pail or container. Use household bleach or disinfectant for odor control. Dispose of used plastic bags by burying them or dumping them into the sewer when service is restored. Another option is a military-type latrine consisting of a trench dug in the earth two to three feet deep. Spread a thin layer of dirt or lime over wastes after each use to control odor, and refill the trench when the emergency period is over.

VOLTAGE-SURGE SUPPRESSORS

Surges or spikes in electrical current can damage electronic equipment, computers, home security systems, and any devices that run on electricity. Protect sensitive electronic equipment with surge protectors that trap a voltage spike before it can do damage. Surge protectors can be plugged into any conventional wall outlet. Be sure to purchase surge protectors that are certified by a nationally recognized testing organization.

▼ Surge protectors trap voltage spikes and can protect sensitive electronic equipment.

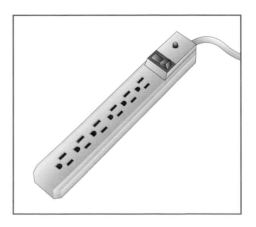

FLOODING

Before a Flood

One of the most important things you can do to protect your home, particularly if the area in which you live is prone to flooding, is to purchase adequate flood insurance. The National Flood Insurance Program (NFIP) guarantees coverage and is administered by the Federal Emergency Management Agency (FEMA). Don't wait until a flood is imminent to purchase flood insurance.

FEMA also suggests that you move appliances or anything of value out of the basement if you live in a flood-prone area and install electric service entrance panels and utility meters above anticipated flood levels.

If a flood is anticipated but the flood waters have not yet arrived, turn off utilities at the main power switch and shut off the main gas valve (if evacuation seems likely). Fill bathtubs, sinks, and other containers with clean, fresh water. Secure outdoor furniture, grills, trash cans, or other possessions with rope, or bring them inside. Move all furniture

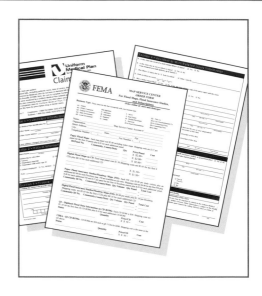

▲ Protect yourself from loss with flood insurance, particularly if you live in an area that is prone to flooding.

and personal belongings to upper floors if time permits.

During a Flood

Family safety is more important than material possessions. Go to the second floor, attic, or even the roof if water begins to rise inside the house. If water is rising, leave personal possessions behind, taking only protective clothing, a portable radio, and a working flashlight. Remain at the highest point in your home until help arrives. Do not try to wade, drive, or swim through water.

After a Flood

FEMA recommends taking the following safety precautions if your home has been affected by flood waters:

- Do not turn utilities back on until your home has been inspected by an electrician and the appropriate utilities service personnel.

- Use a flashlight rather than matches, lighters, or open flames to provide light.

- Do not use water from the pipes until local authorities instruct you that it is safe to do so.

- Use caution when walking around in flood-damaged interiors since water, silt, and debris can make movement dangerous.

- Clean flood damage as soon as possible since flood waters can contaminate surfaces, furniture, and any standing food or water.

- Remove contaminated material and reduce moisture and humidity in the home immediately after the flood waters have receded.

- Have wiring, electrical equipment, and appliances tested for damage before use.

- Call the insurance company that issued your flood insurance policy to report damage.

The National Safety Council contends that flood water can create an indoor air-quality problem by encouraging microorganisms to breed. The NSC makes the following recommendations for controlling excess moisture in the home:

- Open doors and windows, closets, and cabinets to circulate air.

- Use fans to circulate air (if electricity is safely back on).

- Have air conditioners checked before use if they were submerged in flood waters, and then turn on.

- Use dehumidifiers.

- Consider hiring a contractor who specializes in moisture control if water damage was extensive.

EARTHQUAKES

Before an Earthquake

Your emergency plan should include what the family will do in the event of an earthquake. The plan should include the location of a safe place to seek shelter in every room of the house or apartment, perhaps under a sturdy table or desk, and away from windows or tall objects that may topple over.

If you are buying a house, have it evaluated by an architect or building engineer for its ability to withstand an earthquake.

Most existing houses can be reinforced to be more earthquake resistant. Hire an architect or builder to estimate the cost of implementing necessary measures to make the house more resistant to quakes. The foundation's wooden sill plate should be anchored with bolts to the concrete foundation. Crippled walls or wood foundations should be reinforced with sheathing plywood or backing blocks.

If you have a room built over a garage, the wide span of the garage door is a structural weak spot and can collapse during a quake. Plywood panels can brace wood-frame walls against quake stresses. Using drywall screws, install plywood sheathing inside the garage on the walls next to the door opening.

Additions such as porches, balconies, or overhangs should be inspected for adequate support and proper attachment to the house. Inspect slate or tile roofs to be sure they're in good shape and consider lighter roofing material such as asphalt shingles if you are building or remodeling. Chimneys—especially those on houses built before 1934—should be checked by a structural engineer for weakness. Remove any dead tree limbs that are near the house and could fall on it during an earthquake.

Another important thing to consider is the protection of your family and property inside the home should a quake occur.

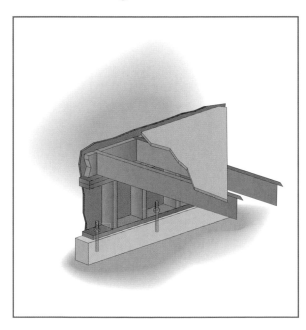

▲ The foundation's wooden sill plate should be anchored to the concrete foundation.

- Anchor tall freestanding furniture, such as bookcases, cabinets, media centers, and the like, to wall studs or wall framing.

- Use metal strapping to hold a water heater firmly to the wall.

- Install wire-reinforced or safety glass or cover ordinary glass with plastic film to prevent shattering.

- Use safety catches on cabinets and drawers to keep contents inside.

- Flexible gas pipes connecting the heater to the gas supply will let the water heater move without breaking the pipe.

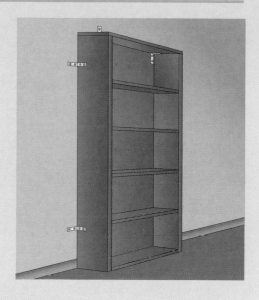

▲ Prepare the interior of the house for an earthquake.

▲ FEMA urges as little movement as possible in the event of an earthquake. Position yourself quickly under a sturdy piece of furniture.

During an Earthquake

The most important consideration during an earthquake is your physical safety. FEMA recommends following these procedures in the event of a quake.

WHAT TO DO DURING AN EARTHQUAKE

■ Move as little as possible to get to a safe position in your home such as under a sturdy table or desk.

■ It is safer to stay where you are; if you are in bed, remain there and cover your head with a pillow.

■ Stay inside until the quake stops and you know it's safe to exit.

■ Keep away from windows.

■ Fire alarms and sprinklers may be activated during an earthquake; check for fires, and if leaving a high-rise, use the stairs.

After an Earthquake

After establishing that you are uninjured, don heavy pants and a long-sleeved shirt as well as sensible shoes to protect yourself from further injury. Extinguish any small fires or call 911 for a fire emergency. Do not turn the gas main off unless you smell gas or think there may be a leak. Clean up any toxic or chemical products, gasoline, or other flammables. Take care when opening closet or cabinet doors since the contents may have shifted. Make a quick inspection of your home for damage and evacuate everyone if you deem it unsafe. Look for weaknesses in walls, ceilings, floors, staircases, and windows. Check the gas, electrical, and plumbing systems for breakage or leaking. Stay away from downed power or broken gas lines. Try to get an update on local emergency conditions and instructions by listening to a battery-operated radio or television. Don't use kerosene lanterns, candles, or matches, and avoid smoking since there may be flammable gases trapped inside the home. (Flashlights or battery-operated lanterns are fine.) Keep telephone lines clear; use them only for life-threatening emergencies. Photograph your home's damage for insurance purposes.

HURRICANES

"Accurate, timely warning and evacuation" are the most important factors in saving lives in the event of a violent hurricane, according to the National Safety Council. Every household should have an emergency plan in place, including procedures to evacuate if a hurricane watch or warning is called. Particularly vulnerable are residents of coastal areas. The National Oceanic and Atmospheric Administration recommends that everyone who lives on the coastline, on an off-shore island, or near a river or flood plain should evacuate when a hurricane threatens. If local authorities recommend that you evacuate, do so.

BEFORE A HURRICANE

- Check emergency supplies kit.
- Protect windows with permanent shutters or plywood panels. Duct tape in an X pattern on window glass will prevent broken shards from flying.
- Inspect rain gutters, down spouts, and roof material for stability.
- Remove dead limbs from trees.
- Secure lawn and garden items in a garage, or anchor to a solid post or tree.
- Have mobile homes tied down with steel cables.
- Secure boat in a safe place.

During a Hurricane Watch

If the threat of a hurricane exists within the next 24 to 36 hours, a hurricane watch will be called. Keep abreast of breaking local news by listening to a battery-operated radio or television. Close and board up windows. Fill bathtubs, sinks, and empty plastic bottles with clean tap water and turn the refrigerator and freezer to the coldest setting. Be prepared to evacuate if such action applies to your situation.

During a Hurricane Warning

If hurricane conditions are expected within 24 hours or less, a hurricane warning will be declared. If you reside in a mobile home, evacuate immediately. Keep your battery-operated radio on constantly for updates in conditions. If you have remained in your home, keep away from windows, skylights, and doors. Move to the lowest level of the house, such as a basement, if you have one, or the first floor. Do not attempt to go outside until authorities indicate that the storm is over and it is safe to do so. Remember that there is a quiet center, or eye, in a hurricane so that the storm passes in two phases.

If you are outside when a windstorm hits and you don't have time to move indoors, lie face down in a ditch with your hands over your head. This position will help you avoid head injuries from flying objects.

LIGHTNING

The safest refuges from lightning include buildings that are equipped with lightning protection, large steel-framed buildings, cars, and large framed buildings with wood floors. When lightning strikes in your area, avoid talking on land-line telephones, bathing, doing laundry, watching television, and using electronic equipment. Don't stand near open windows or doors or come into contact with metal pipes such as hot water pipes or plumbing drain stacks.

Outside locations to avoid during lightning storms include unprotected (by lightning equipment) shelters in parks or on golf courses, open fields, lone trees, trees in woods, or wire fencing. Don't swim. Dismount from your horse, bicycle, golf cart, or lawn tractor.

If you are caught in an open area, kneel down and bend low to the ground. Touch the ground with only your knees and feet. Keep your arms folded at your sides and do not touch your hands to your knees.

WINTER WEATHER

As previously discussed, all households should prepare an emergency supplies kit in the event of isolation in the home or the need for evacuation. Supplies should be sufficient to ensure human survival for a minimum of three days. If you reside in an area where winter storms are common, keep a supply of rock salt on hand to melt ice on sidewalks and driveways.

Familiarize yourself with weather terms used in forecasts. A winter storm watch indicates the possibility of a winter storm while a winter storm warning cites an imminent or occurring storm. A prediction of an approaching blizzard means that falling and/or blowing snow, winds of 35 mph or greater, and reduced visibility to one-quarter mile or less are expected. The ability to move about or travel is

Plan ahead to protect yourself from the potential hazards of winter.

greatly diminished during a blizzard because of drifting snow, extreme cold, and wind-chill factors. Never leave shelter during blizzard conditions.

FEMA suggests, that you prepare for possible isolation in your home by having an emergency supplies kit on hand and by

- Stocking emergency heating equipment and fuel, including seasoned firewood if you have a fireplace or wood-burning stove.

- Maintaining working fire extinguishers in the home.

- Winterizing your home by insulating walls and attics; caulking doors and windows; and installing storm windows or sheets of plastic.

Contaminants in the Environment

▲ The EPA has classified secondhand tobacco smoke as a carcinogen.

ENVIRONMENTAL TOBACCO SMOKE (ETS)

The mixture of particles released into the air from a burning cigarette, pipe, or cigar—as well as the smoke exhaled by a smoker—contains more than 40 compounds known to cause cancer in humans. This "secondhand smoke" is classified as a Group A carcinogen by the U.S. Environmental Protection Agency (EPA) and causes approximately 3,000 lung cancer deaths of non-smoking adults per year. According to the EPA other negative health effects linked to exposure to environmental tobacco smoke include:

- Increased risk of pneumonia and bronchitis in infants and young children.

- An increase in the buildup of fluid in the middle ear in children under 18 months of age (which can lead to ear infections).

- Slightly reduced lung function, especially in older children.

- An increase in the number of asthma episodes and in the severity of symptoms in children with asthma.

- A propensity for nonasthmatic children to develop the disease.

The National Safety Council urges residents not to smoke in the home, particularly if children are present. Do not allow caregivers to smoke in the home or around children.

ASBESTOS

Most of the health risk associated with asbestos today involves insulation materials made before 1970 that deteriorate or are damaged when removed. Asbestos is a mineral fiber that was commonly used as a fire retardant in construction products. When asbestos fibers get into the air and are breathed, they can accumulate in the lungs and present an increased risk of cancer.

Is It Asbestos?

Products today are generally not made of asbestos. If a product does contain asbestos, it must be so labeled. If the material is not labeled, it must be analyzed by a qualified professional to determine asbestos content. Building products manufactured before 1970 may contain asbestos fibers. According to the National Safety Council, any of the following products may include asbestos if they were produced before 1970: pipe and furnace insulation, asbestos and cement shingles, siding, millboard, floor tiles, vinyl-sheet floor backing, tile adhesives, soundproofing or decorative material, patching and joint compound, fireproof gloves and stove-top pads, automotive brake pads and linings, clutch facings and gaskets.

The EPA recommends that asbestos be handled by a professional since the material is more hazardous when disturbed. Asbestos material that is in good condition is best left alone. If you are having material tested, let a professional analyst extract the sample since, once again, the material is safer dormant than disturbed.

LEAD

Lead is a toxin found in paint made before 1978, dust, soil, water, ceramics, home remedies, dyes, and some cosmetics. Children are at the greatest risk of lead poisoning, and most are exposed to lead in their own homes. The National Safety Council offers the following guidelines for protecting your family and home from lead toxicity.

If your home or apartment building was built before 1978, have the paint tested. You should also have a technician check to see whether your home contains lead-contaminated dust.

Use lead-safe work practices when remodeling or renovating if your home contains lead paint. Here is how your children, pets, and personal belongings can be protected from exposure:

Lead paint was used in homes until 1978 and should be the greatest cause for concern when considering lead poisoning.

■ Keep the paint in your home in top condition.

■ Clean up lead-contaminated dust by using soapy water and a mop.

■ Have your drinking water checked for hazardous levels of lead.

■ Eat foods rich in iron, calcium, and zinc such as eggs, raisins, legumes, milk, cheese, and lean red meats.

■ Wash your child's hands frequently and do not allow her to play in dust or soil that may be contaminated.

■ Do not use ceramic pottery dishware unless you are certain it is lead-free.

■ Alcoholic beverages should not be stored in lead crystal decanters.

■ Cover bare soil with mulch, grass, or an alternative covering.

(See the section on lead poisoning in the "Safeguarding Infants and Children" chapter.)

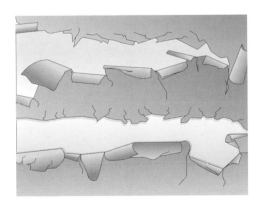

▲ Peeling lead paint and lead paint dust are extremely toxic to children and adults.

BIOLOGICAL CONTAMINANTS

Biological contaminants such as bacteria, mold, mildew, viruses, dust mites, pollen, and animal dander can negatively affect human health if they become airborne or infect surfaces inside the home. Since biological contaminants are living organisms, they need a source of food and moisture to thrive. Bathrooms, damp basements, wet building materials, flood-damaged appliances—even air conditioners and dehumidifiers—can provide a receptive environment for biological contaminants.

Effect on Health

Biological contaminants may cause allergic reactions, respiratory irritation, and asthmatic symptoms. The toxins emitted by some molds and mildews can cause tissue and organ damage. Of particular vulnerability to biological contaminants are children and anyone with allergies, respiratory illnesses, asthma, or lung disease. Symptoms of exposure include coughing and sneezing, shortness of breath, disorientation, tiredness, fever, and digestive-track problems, according to the National Safety Council's fact sheet on biological contaminants.

Limiting Exposure to Contaminants

The NSC suggests taking the following actions to limit your exposure to biological contaminants:

- Equip kitchens and bathrooms with exhaust fans vented to the outdoors.

- Use a dehumidifier to maintain a humidity level of between 30 and 50 percent.

- Water-damaged carpets, upholstery, and furniture should be thoroughly cleaned and dried.

- Vacuum and dust your home regularly to keep dust mites, animal dander, and pollen in check.

- Don't allow moisture to accumulate in attics, basements, or crawl spaces.

- Keep air conditioners, heat pumps, furnaces, and humidifiers clean, and change the filters frequently.

CARBON MONOXIDE

Carbon monoxide is a toxic, odorless, and colorless gas produced as a by product of fuel burning heating and cooking equipment, vehicles, and generators. Combustion appliances such as space heaters, ovens and stoves, furnaces, fireplaces, and water heaters are often fueled by natural gas, fuel oil, kerosene, wood, or coal, and—though generally safe when used correctly—can emit dangerous levels of carbon monoxide if improperly installed maintained, or poorly ventilated. The exhaust from gas-burning vehicles and generators also contains high levels of carbon monoxide.

Carbon monoxide can be deadly. Four hundred people died of carbon monoxide poisoning in the year 2000, according to the National Safety Council. Interfering with the passage of oxygen in the blood, carbon monoxide affects coordination, causes fatigue, headaches, and dizziness, and in very high levels can kill you.

HOW TO PREVENT CARBON MONOXIDE POISONING

- Equip all sleeping areas in the home with UL-tested carbon-monoxide alarms and test them once a month.

- Kerosene heaters, furnaces, chimneys, and air-conditioning and venting systems should be inspected once a year by a qualified professional.

- Never turn on the oven or stove top to heat your home.

- Never burn a charcoal grill or hibachi inside the home or garage.

- Do not run a gasoline-burning vehicle in the garage, even with the garage door open.

- Properly ventilate when using a space heater: keep the door to the room open and leave a window open slightly.

- Use exhaust fans in the kitchen over gas stoves and ranges.

- When buying an existing home, have the cooking and heating systems checked by a licensed technician for proper installation and operating integrity.

- Purchase wood stoves that meet or exceed EPA emission standards and burn only aged or cured wood.

- Always open the flue in the fireplace before starting a fire.

Insurance Issues

Up-to-date homeowner's insurance is a critical part of protecting yourself from property loss. Generally, homeowner's insurance does not include coverage due to damage from a flood or an earthquake. Extra coverage is required and should be obtained before a flood or earthquake occurs. Make sure you understand what your homeowner's insurance covers and what it does not, and seek additional coverage relevant to the likelihood of natural disasters in your area.

The Federal Emergency Management Agency (FEMA) provides information about flood insurance guaranteed through the National Flood Insurance Program (NFIP) at their Web site www.fema.gov/nfip. Most insurance companies can provide a separate earthquake policy, the cost of which will depend on the probability of a quake occurring in your area.

In addition to insuring the house and furnishings, be aware of the limitations of basic coverage of expensive or irreplaceable items such as jewelry, furs, electronic equipment, artwork, or collections. Riders that provide extra coverage will increase the premium you pay but will also compensate you more adequately for loss. Keep receipts for expensive items purchased and have any collections appraised. Take these receipts and appraisals to your insurance agent and have him or her attach a rider that extends coverage to the extra items.

LOWER INSURANCE COSTS

Many insurance providers offer savings on insurance premiums if your home is made disaster-resistant or more secure. The addition of storm shutters, smoke detectors, sprinkler systems, and burglar alarms may reduce premiums. By shopping around for an insurer, purchasing homeowner's, auto, and additional coverage from one insurer, and staying with the same insurer for a lengthy period, you can save on insurance costs.

PROOF OF LOSS

If the total contents of your home were lost in a disaster such as a fire or a flood, could you prove ownership of every item you lost? In the aftermath of such an emergency, could you even remember every item to list? To be sure you will be fully compensated for every item, make a list and also keep a photographic record of your personal property.

Make a comprehensive written checklist of all your household possessions. Include the brand name or make and model number of every appliance, camera, and piece of electronic gear. List all suits, topcoats, furs, and sports gear.

Obtain written appraisals from experts for valuable items and make several copies available for insurance agents and your records. Use a quality still, digital, or video camera to make a photo record of each room. Take clear photos in which every item of value is displayed. Open closet doors and photograph the entire contents since even a modest wardrobe can add up to a replacement cost of several thousand dollars.

Digital cameras allow you to make an electronic record of your possessions. If you are using a digital camera, or have otherwise digitized your photos, you can email copies of the

images to yourself, creating a file accessible on your server's page from any computer. If your PC or laptop is destroyed, a photographic record is still available on your electronic mail server's hard drive.

If you use a still or video camera, make several copies of the photos or videotapes. Keep one set of photo records at home, in your own files. Keep backup records—in a safe-deposit box or home of a relative—in case your home records are lost or destroyed.

▲ Digital images of your possessions can be saved to a file outside the home for insurance purposes.

Contractor/Repair Fraud

The aftermath of a disaster is a vulnerable time for those affected, particularly if property has been lost or damaged. Although the majority of contractors that offer inspection and repair services are responsible and fair, as with any industry, there are exceptions to the rule. To protect yourself from the unscrupulous few, precaution is in order.

When procuring the services of a contractor for disaster repair, remember that much of the damage to your home may be difficult to see. For example, earthquakes can crack or distort foundations and footings. Damage may appear to be cosmetic but may in fact be serious enough to require the building to be condemned. An architect or building engineer can determine the extent of the damage. An unscrupulous contractor might make superficial repairs costing a great deal of money without addressing more serious construction issues. Don't rush the decision to enter into a repair contract, and be wary of any contractor who stresses immediate availability or the urgency to sign a contract.

Be vigilant about checking a contractor's financial and job references. Ask friends, relatives, and coworkers for the names of responsible contracting firms. Hire a local contractor who is fully licensed, bonded, and insured. Get at least three separate, written bids.

It's a good idea to put everything in writing. This includes a description of the job, start and finish dates, a material specifications sheet that includes the make, model, and/or type of materials that will be used, and the contractor's license number and insurance certificate. Be sure that every detail of the agreement is in the written contract.

Don't advance the contractor a large sum of money up front. Make a reasonable down payment and spell out in writing exactly how the balance of the fee will be paid as materials are delivered and work progresses.

▲ Put estimates and job descriptions
in writing when engaging a contractor
in repair work.

5

Crime

Prevention

Although the U.S. Department of Justice cites a 20-year decline (since 1973) in the rate of property crimes nationally, law-enforcement experts still urge residents to take home security precautions rather than rely on optimistic statistics to keep family and property safe. Burglary and theft are crimes of opportunity, so the more difficult you make getting into your home, the more likely it is that a burglar will go elsewhere. Keep in mind that burglars don't want to be seen while breaking in, so they are most likely to select a means of entry that is hidden from view: a rear entrance, a window shrouded by shrubs or trees, or a side door not visible from the street. While trees and fences offer homeowners a sense of privacy, they also give burglars the shield they need to gain illegal entry.

Remember too that the fastest way into a house is through the door, so this is where most burglars start. Securing doors and windows with theft-resistant locks and keeping doors and windows locked are the most important things you can do to prevent theft.

Protecting Your Home

It's a good idea to take periodic tours of your home to check for areas vulnerable to entry.

DOORS
Front door should have a high-quality entry lockset and dead-bolt, as well as a heavy-duty security chain.

▲ A security chain should be installed below the main lock.

Exterior doors should be solid hardwood or metal.

Hinges installed on the inside, with nonremovable pins, prevent the door from being removed.

Apartment dwellers should consider installing multipoint locks that insert bolts into all four sides of the door simultaneously.

Back and side doors should be equipped with high-quality dead-bolt locks.

Glass windows or panels on doors should be reinforced with grilles or Plexiglas.

Sliding glass doors must be fitted with special locks, a dowel, or a pin that prevents easy entry.

If your property has a side gate, lock it to prevent burglars from carrying away bulky items.

WINDOWS

Windows on the first level are best supplied with keyed locking devices or pins that lock the window shut or allow the window to be locked into a position with no more than 6 inches of open space. (Any window used as an emergency fire exit should not require a key but should be equipped with removable grilles or bars.)

Second-story windows should have key-operated locks installed.

A window accessible by a fire escape, balcony, or roof requires an extra security device, such as a gate or grill that is removable in the event of a fire.

Always lock or bolt skylights to secure them.

Install bolt locks on the top and bottom sashes of French windows to prevent the windows from being pushed in.

Secure leaded or stained-glass windows or panels that are vulnerable to breakage with grilles, gates, Plexiglas, or exterior shutters.

GARAGES AND SHEDS

Equip outbuilding doors with heavy-duty door locks or padlocks and hasps; choose case-hardened padlocks with a ⅜-inch shackle resistant to being forced; install padlock plates with bolts rather than screws and make sure the bolts are inaccessible when the padlock is closed.

Porches, patios, side entrances, and areas around outbuildings should be illuminated.

Security-conscious Habits

You can reduce the likelihood of burglary by practicing security-conscious habits. Close and lock all doors and windows, even if you are away for only a short time. Keep doors locked when you are home, and open windows only if they are installed with security gates or locking devices that prevent them from being opened more than 6 inches. Use lighting to illuminate your home when you are away and to brighten dark areas around the perimeter of your house.

Close the curtains at night and leave on a light that is attached to an automatic timer. Don't leave tempting items such as bicycles, barbecue grills, tools, or furniture on your lawn or porch. Keep garage doors closed and locked.

Do everything you can to make your home appear occupied when you are away: leave lights and a radio on timers and have the lawn mowed and newspapers and mail collected. Ladders and tools should be locked away so as not to provide burglars with a means to access your home.

Precautions

LOCKS

Door Locks

Install strong locks and bolts on all exterior doors, since doors are particularly vulnerable to burglars. Older, worn locks should be replaced with newer, higher-quality units. If you are an apartment dweller, it is imperative that you change the lock/cylinder since you have no idea who might have access to the key.

The front door needs a strong lock, particularly for periods when you are not at home and it will not be bolted from inside. Back and side doors need extra protection since they are often targeted because they cannot be seen from the street; an intruder may try to open them with force.

Install good-quality dead-bolt cylinder locks or mortise locks in all exterior doors. If purchasing a dead-bolt cylinder lock, look for a bolt that extends at least 1 inch beyond the edge of the door when in the locked position. Make sure the lock has a case-hardened cylinder guard, steel inserts, a reinforced strike plate, and tie screws a minimum of 3 inches long that secure from the inside.

A lock whose operation requires a key from both the inside and outside (a double-cylinder lock) may be a good idea for side and back doors. Without a key, a thief will have difficulty removing bulky property from the rear of your home and will be forced to leave through a window or the front door. Double cylinder locks also prevent a burglar from breaking the glass window in a door and reaching in and unlocking the door. (Since double-cylinder locks can be operated only with a key, they can be hazardous when used in doors that are the only means of egress in the event of fire and may even be prohibited by some city and/or county ordinances.)

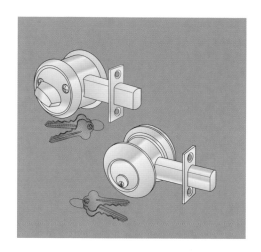

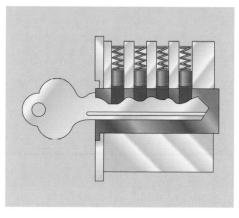

▲ Double-cylinder locks require a key from both inside and outside.

Window Locks

The standard "thumb-turn" locks found on most double-hung windows are a mild deterrent for the average burglar, who can open them easily through a broken pane of glass. Locks operated by a removable key are the most secure. Since leaving the key in the lock decreases security, it is important that every member of the household know where window lock keys are kept and how to use them. The installation of locks and protective grilles should always be considered in tandem with your emergency exit plan.

Dual Screws, Sash Stops, and Pins

An inexpensive but effective way of safeguarding windows is to immobilize movement of the sashes with a dual screw, nail, or pin that passes through both meeting rails. A hole is drilled through the inner meeting rail into the outer one, and then a dual screw (with bolt), nail, or pin is inserted until it is flush with the window frame. A second set of holes to permit the window to be partially open allows for ventilation.

◀ Casement locks have removable keys. Be sure that family members can locate keys in the event of emergency.

▲ Window locks should be installed at key points for maximum security.

GRILLES AND BARS

Windows at ground level, within 24 feet of ground level, or accessible by fire escapes, balconies, or rooftops need extra protection. Once again you must consider how that extra protection fits in with your emergency exit plan. Bars, grilles, gates, and glass block are effective means for preventing unwanted entry but also may inhibit family members from getting out quickly in the event of an emergency. Bars installed to prevent passage should have openings of no more than 6 inches. Window grilles, gates, or guards can be purchased with hinges or latches to ensure quick removal.

BURGLAR ALARMS

A burglar alarm can provide extra security, acting as one more level of deterrent to burglars who seek easy entry. But they shouldn't be considered burglarproof and are certainly no substitute for quality locks and security-conscious habits. The alarm system must be reliable and be used dependably by all family members. The consistent peel of false alarms will soon be ignored by neighbors. Police departments in many communities will not respond to an alarm unless summoned by an individual. Consider informing police in your area of the names of two key-holders in the event that the alarm is engaged.

There are two basic kinds of alarm system: passive types that detect an intruder's presence in the home, and perimeter units that protect doors, windows, and other points of entry. A combination of features will provide the best protection.

A Typical Alarm System

Control Unit

The control unit is the central part of the system, since the detectors are attached to it and it is from the control unit that the signal is passed to a bell, siren, or other notification device. The control unit must be set to permit family members enough time to come and go. One option permits door contacts or sensors to be activated in selected zones, such as those on doors and windows in the downstairs portion of the house, while disarming sensors where family activity continues. A tamperproof control unit will prevent anyone from disarming it without the proper key or digital code. The control unit should have a rechargeable battery in case of power failure.

Detectors

Magnetic contacts or detectors trigger the alarm when someone opening a door or window breaks the contact. Other types of detectors are sensitive to movement and vibration. To sense the difference between an intruder and ordinary, external stimulus, detectors must be installed and calibrated accurately.

Scanning Devices

The infrared sensors on a scanning device detect movement in a wide expanse. One advantage is that they can be positioned to ignore the presence of pets.

Although usually connected to a central control unit, independent, battery-operated sensors are available.

Alarm

A bell or siren installed on an outside wall is activated when signaled from the control unit. After a prescribed period of time, the alarm turns off. Some alarms contain lights that continue to flash; some automatically rearm. If you choose a burglar alarm monitored by a security service, a warning is transmitted directly to a monitoring center. No matter what type of alarm you choose, make sure that the alarm is triggered not only via detectors or scanners but also when any attempt is made to dismantle the alarm directly.

Do-It-Yourself Alarm Systems

There are several alarm systems available for the do-it-yourselfer. Before installation, check with the supplier of the equipment to ensure proper placement of sensors and detectors. Most important is that the control unit of the system be tamperproof. Wireless systems simplify installation as there is no need for extensive wiring; outbuildings can still be monitored. Self-contained systems plug into any outlet and can be moved as needed.

Motion Detectors

Using infrared sensors to monitor the presence of moving objects, animals, or people, motion detector lights are an inexpensive and effective safety precaution. Quite simply, a light turns on when movement is sensed from below. The detector can be adjusted to determine the amount of "heat" needed to activate the sensor and turn on the light. On sensitive settings, the light will be activated by the presence of a small dog or cat. A second adjustment permits the light to be activated at a certain level of darkness. A third control determines the length of time the light will stay on when triggered. Motion detectors can play an important role in denying burglars the cover they need to gain illegal entry.

Automatic Timer Switches

An automatic timer switch—plugged into an ordinary electrical wall socket—can turn lights, radios, and televisions on and off, giving the outward appearance that someone is home at all times. You can set the program to turn appliances on and off several times throughout the day or night. Sophisticated models can be set for different times every day of the week.

Door Viewer

A peephole lets you identify visitors before opening the door. Install a wide-angled viewer that permits you to see beside the door as well as the floor beneath it. Purchase a viewer that fits any door thickness.

▲ A door viewer allows you to identify callers.

Identity Theft

Identity theft is a serious crime in which your name, social security number, bank account or credit card number, or any other personal information, is stolen and used without your permission and with the intent of committing fraud or other crimes. Victims of identity theft can incur financial loss or damage to their credit rating; they can be refused education or housing loans or even be charged with crimes not committed.

The Federal Trade Commission has an informative Web site (www.consumer.gov/idtheft) dedicated to protecting consumers from the serious crime of identity theft. The FTC recommends taking the following precautions to minimize the risk of identity theft:

- Create passwords for your credit card, bank, and telephone accounts.

- Avoid using passwords that contain obvious choices such as your mother's maiden name, your birth date, or the last four digits of your social security number.

- Protect the personal information in your home if you have roommates, outside help, or service personnel in the home.

- Never give out personal information over the telephone or Internet unless you initiated the contact.

- Deposit outgoing mail at the post office collection box rather than in an unsecured mailbox.

- Have your mail held at the post office when you go on vacation.

- Destroy all bank statements, credit card receipts, offers, and applications before throwing them in the garbage.

- Before providing personal information on applications, ask how it will be used.

- Do not give out your social security number unless absolutely necessary.

- Carry only those credit and debit cards that you need.

- Update virus protection software frequently.

- Use only a secure browser when submitting information over the Internet.

- Avoid storing financial information on your laptop.

- Use "strong" passwords created from a combination of letters, numbers, and symbols.

- Don't use automatic log-in features that save your name and password.

- Always log off when completing a transaction on an Internet site.

- Delete any personal information before getting rid of hardware.

- Don't download files from unfamiliar addresses or click on hyperlinks unknown to you.

- Install a firewall to limit outside access to your computer, particularly if you have a high-speed connection to the Internet.

WHAT TO DO IF YOUR IDENTITY IS STOLEN

The Federal Trade Commission suggests that you immediately take the following steps if you think your personal information has been tampered with or stolen:

- Place a "fraud alert" on your credit file with any of the three major credit bureaus.

- Close any accounts that you know or suspect to have been accessed or opened without your permission.

- File a police report.

- File a complaint with the FTC.

Personal Safety

Only you can decide whether having a chemical irritant spray (such as mace or pepper spray), a stun gun, or a firearm available in your home is the right course to take. Most law-enforcement agencies across the country recommend careful consideration of the facts before purchasing any personal safety device. A major concern is that the device may be used against you or a family member. There may also be civil or criminal ramifications from the use of these devices. Consider the following before arming yourself with a firearm, stun gun, or chemical irritant spray.

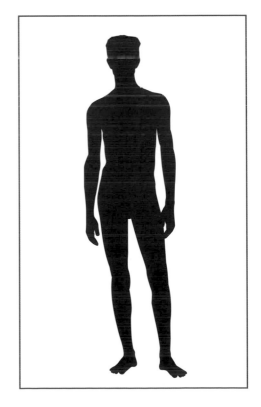

HANDGUNS

Firearms represent a potential hazard to family members, particularly children.

Firearms are frequently stolen by burglars and used in subsequent crimes.

The licensed owner of a handgun may be legally responsible for injuries or deaths caused by its use or misuse.

An intruder may take possession of the gun and use it against you or a family member.

The proper use of a gun requires special skills acquired through coursework and practice.

Gun owners may develop a false sense of security that weakens their commitment to practicing other home security habits.

CHEMICAL IRRITANT SPRAYS

Chemical sprays are meant to be carried in the hand and used in the event of a personal assault. They can be effective only if immediately available at the onset of the attack and are therefore unhelpful buried in a purse or drawer. Individuals with mental-health disorders—or those under the influence of drugs or alcohol—may not be affected by chemical irritants, and if the spray does nothing to impede the attacker, the severity of the attack may be heightened. As with any weapon, control is key: sprays can just as easily be used on you. Finally, for the spray to be effective, you must be in close proximity to your assailant, which is the last place you want to be.

STUN GUNS

Many of the same considerations one makes about chemical sprays should be used before purchasing a stun gun. Small, battery-operated weapons that deliver a high-voltage shock, stun guns must be placed in direct contact with your assailant's skin or body. Since you must be in close proximity to your attacker, odds are increased that the weapon will be taken away and used against you. If your attacker has on heavy clothing, the stun gun may have little effect.

6

Plumbing

Turning Off Water

Whether you live in a house or in an apartment, the city or the country, you should know how to stop the flow of water in your home. An emergency may arise that calls for the cessation of water flow; it could be a broken pipe, a leaking plumbing fixture, or some sort of natural disaster during which the utilities need to be turned off. Find out whether the water valves can be turned by hand or will require a wrench, if a wrench is required keep the correct size wrench handy.

WATER METER VALVE

If you reside in a house in the city or suburbs, most likely the local water company supplies water to all the homes in the neighborhood through the water main. The meter that records water consumption for the supplier is most likely found just inside the basement wall closest to the street. Find out where the water meter is in your house. Water meters are made of brass, about 6 inches in diameter, and have a housing that contains a dial and counter similar to the odometer in your car. To shut off all water flow throughout the house, find the main valve on the side of the meter where the street pipe enters the house. Turn the main valve—or "gate valve" as it is known—clockwise; if there are two valves, turn off the valve on the supply side of the meter.

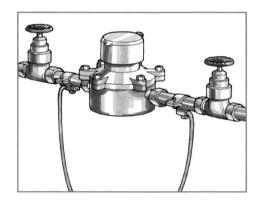

▲ Water meter valve.

PLUMBING FIXTURE VALVES

In addition to the main water valve, there are often shutoff valves at each plumbing fixture, such as the sink, toilet, bathtub, washer, and water heater. If you live in an apartment, you probably won't have access to the main water valve and can shut off the flow of the water to individual fixtures. Separate shutoff valves also enable you to work on individual fixtures without turning off the flow of water to the entire house. Look for shutoff valves under the sink in the bathroom, under the kitchen sink, on the incoming cold water pipe on the water heater, and beneath the water tank or closet behind the toilet bowl.

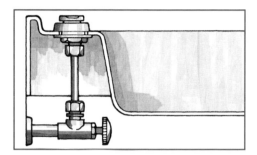

Locate the valve to the fixture and turn it clockwise. A faucet will have two shutoffs: one for cold water and one for hot.

WELL PUMP
Rural residents who get their water supply from a private well should be able to locate and shut off the well pump switch or valve, located at the top of the well pump. Alternatively you can turn off the valve on the supply pipe from the well to the house.

◄ Shutoff valve under the sink.

Emergency Repairs

FROZEN AND SPLIT PIPES
In colder climates, pipes located in exterior walls, crawl spaces, and attics are often subject to freezing. The best preventive measure is to insulate these pipes. Even insulated pipes can freeze when exposed to drafts of extremely cold air. When pipes freeze, a plug of ice forms in a small section of the pipe and expands, swelling the pipe, and, in most cases, rupturing the pipe

▲ Frozen pipes are easily split.

wall. Even a well-protected pipe may crack after years of use.

A sure sign that a pipe has frozen is that no water passes through the pipe to the faucets nearest the freeze. You will often be able to feel along the pipe and locate the frozen area.

If the pipe has not yet ruptured, use a portable hair dryer to warm the frozen area until water flows again to the nearest faucet. Move a hair dryer back and forth over a wide area so the pipe will thaw evenly. Once the pipe has thawed, you should wrap it with insulation.

If you can see that the pipe has already split, you will need to drain the system before thawing the frozen area. Once the area has thawed, you will need some sort of emergency repair.

REPAIR LEAKS TEMPORARILY

The flow of water should be turned off before beginning any repair. If you have access to a plumbing supplier, the easiest repair solution for a split pipe is a sleeve-type repair coupling. Available in a number of standard sizes, repair couplings consist of two metal halves that are hinged on one side and bolted together on the other. A rubber sleeve fits inside, wrapping completely around the pipe.

INSTALLING A SLEEVE-TYPE REPAIR COUPLING

- Clean the affected pipe with a wire brush or sandpaper.
- Fit the rubber sleeve around the pipe, seam opposite the leak.
- Fit the metal halves of the collar over the sleeve and tighten halves the together.

If conventional repair materials are unavailable, you can sometimes create a temporary patch using materials found around the house or at an all-night service station. You'll need a piece of tire inner tube or a section of old garden hose, and a few radiator hose clamps.

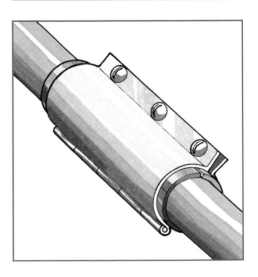

▲ Sleeve-type repair coupling.

MAKING A TEMPORARY PATCH

■ Wrap the inner tube (or garden hose) around the split pipe several times.

■ Clamp it in place with radiator clamps.

■ Make sure clamps fall on either side of the split.

■ Tighten clamps firmly in place.

A general purpose epoxy kit may enable you to create an epoxy patch to temporarily repair a split pipe. Such kits consist of two sticks of putty that are mixed together. An epoxy patch must cure properly, usually 24 hours, before the water can be turned on.

EPOXY PATCH REPAIR

■ Clean the pipe area with sandpaper and alcohol.

■ Knead together the two sticks of putty provided in the kit. (You will have approximately 15 minutes to work before the mixture sets.)

■ Press the epoxy putty around the pipe.

■ Smooth ends with a damp cloth until epoxy forms a seamless bond around the pipe.

■ Make sure epoxy patch extends several inches beyond either side of the split.

■ Do not put full pressure in the pipes for at least 24 hours after application.

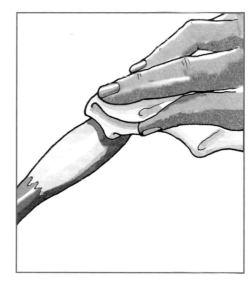

▲ You can create a temporary patch using common household items.

▲ Epoxy patch repair kits are available at most hardware stores.

Water heaters are fairly simple appliances, but when problems arise, they can present an array of confusing symptoms. Because malfunctions can occur in any part of your hot water system, don't limit your investigation to the heater alone.

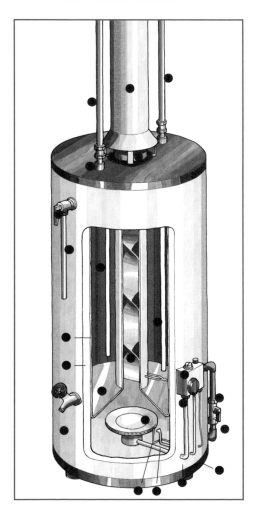

PROBLEMS INSIDE THE TANK

An aging water system can carry sediment into a tank, or sediment may collect in flakes of calcium and lime. In electric models, sediment-covered heating elements will burn out quickly. In gas water heaters, sediment accumulates in the bottom of the tank and forms a barrier between the heat source and the water. Not only does sediment make your heater very inefficient, but air bubbles created by the heat percolate through the sediment and cause a continuous rumbling sound. If your electric heater burns up lower elements frequently, or if your heater rumbles, sediment may be the culprit.

To remove sediment, drain as much water as possible from the tank. Then turn on the water supply and allow the new water to flush through the drain valve for a few minutes.

◄ Basic parts of a gas water-heater

1 Vent
2 Cold water inlet
3 Hot water outlet
4 Flue hat
5 Union
6 Relief valve
7 Discharge pipe
8 Anode rod
9 Water
10 Tank
11 Dip Tube
12 Insulation
13 Flue Baffle
14 Gas control
15 Gas pipe
16 Temperature Control
17 Gas valve—
18 Burner
19 Draincock
20 Thermocouple lead
21 Pilot line
22 Burner supply
23 Thermocouple

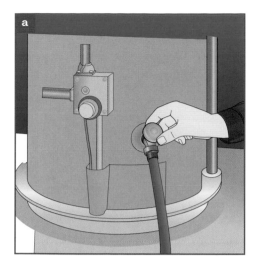

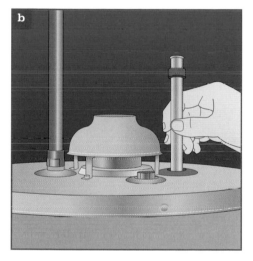

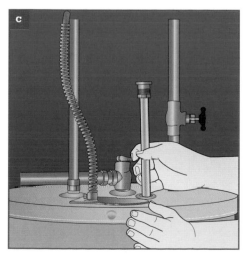

A dip tube is a plastic pipe that delivers cold water to the heat source near the tank bottom. Occasionally a dip tube will slip through the cold water inlet and fall into the tank. When this happens, cold water entering the tank is drawn through the hot water outlet without being heated. To replace a dip tube, disconnect the inlet pipe from the tank. Slide a new dip tube into the fitting and reconnect the inlet pipe.

New water heaters are equipped with magnesium anode rods that prevent rust from developing in the porcelain tank lining. An anode rod draws rust and corrosion to itself rather than allowing it to settle in the tank lining. Usually trouble-free, magnesium rods may become ineffective if the water has a high concentration of dissolved mineral salts. If this occurs, the water will have a gassy odor or taste and the magnesium rod should be replaced with an aluminum rod.

A relief valve prevents a heater from exploding if the thermostat gets stuck. When pressure builds

▲ To remove sediment, drain water from the tank using an ordinary hose.
▲ Slide a new dip tube into the fitting.
◄ Anode rods can be unscrewed and removed from the tank.

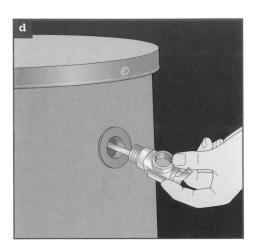

▲ Remove the old relief valve and replace with a new one.

and the water gets too hot, the relief valve opens until pressure is equalized. However, the spring mechanism in some valves weakens with age and the valves release water with any slight variation in pressure. To correct this, simply remove the old valve and thread in a new one.

GAS WATER HEATER PROBLEMS

A typical gas water heater consists of a steel tank, a layer of insulation, and a sheet metal jacket. The bottom of the tank is heated by a fixed gas burner that is controlled by a thermocouple and a regulator valve. To vent excess heat and noxious fumes, a gas heater tank is equipped with a hollow tube, through its center, that connects to a house flue.

Flame Burns Orange

If the flame in your gas water heater burns orange and jumps and pops, the system may not be getting a sufficient supply of secondary air. An orange flame means higher operating costs. Be sure that the heater has a sufficient supply of combustion air by opening doors in confined areas or by installing louvered vents in the doors.

Clogged Flue

A clogged flue is caused by rust or debris that accumulates at tight bends in the flue pipe. A serious health hazard, a clogged flue may force deadly carbon gases into the living quarters. An easy way to check that the flue is working properly is to place a burning match or burning piece of cardboard near the flue hat while the heater is on. The smoke should be drawn into the flue. To locate an obstruction, turn the heater to pilot and disassemble the vent pipes. Inspect and clean each piece of pipe and then reassemble the flue.

Heater Burning Unevenly or Not at All

If your heater is burning unevenly or not burning at all, it may have dirt in the pilot line or burner line. To clean these lines, disconnect them from the regulator and slide a thin wire through each line. Blow air through the lines. If dirt is lodged in the gas control valve, call a plumber. Control valves are delicate mechanisms that can be dangerous if serviced improperly.

Pilot Light Out

If the pilot light on your gas water heater is out or won't burn, the thermocouple may need to be replaced. The thermocouple is a thick copper wire that has a heat sensor on one end and a plug on the other. Heat from the pilot flame sends a tiny millivolt charge through the wire, which causes the plug to open the control valve. When a thermocouple's sensor burns out, the heater's magnetic safety valve remains closed and the pilot light won't burn. To replace a thermocouple, turn off the gas and dis-

connect the entire burner assembly from the control valve. Remove the thermocouple from its retainer clip near the pilot and snap in a replacement. Be sure to position the sensor directly in line with the pilot flame. Reconnect the burner assembly to the control valve.

If You Smell Gas

If you smell a strong gas odor, it's likely there is a dangerous gas leak. Leave the house immediately and call your gas or utility company.

If you smell only a light trace of gas, it may be a leaky pipe joint. To find the leak, brush every joint with a mixture of dish detergent and warm water. Soap bubbles will appear around the leaky joint. Turn off the gas at the meter. Bleed the line at the union located above the heater and ventilate the area. Take apart the leaking joint and clean the fitting and pipe thoroughly with a wire brush. Reassemble the parts with pipe-joint compound. Tighten all the joints. Turn on the gas, bleed the air from the line, and retest all the new joints with soap and water.

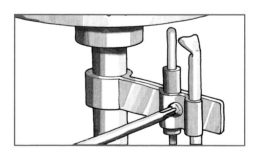

▲ **Loosen clip screw to remove thermocouple.**

► Test for gas leaks with a mixture of detergent and water.

ELECTRIC WATER HEATER PROBLEMS

If your electric water heater fails, first check for tripped circuit breakers (or burned-out fuses) at the main service panel. If the problem is not in the service panel, go to the heater. Remove the access panels and press the reset button on each thermostat and listen for a ticking noise caused by expansion as elements begin to heat. If this fails to produce hot water, the problem may be in the wiring, thermostats, or elements.

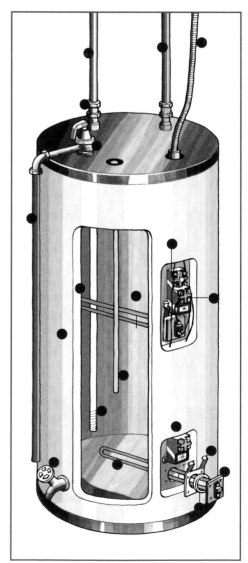

Basic parts of an electric water heater

1 Cold water inlet
2 Hot water outlet
3 Union
4 Power cable
5 Relief valve
6 Discharge pipe
7 Insulation
8 Tank
9 High limit switch
10 Upper element
11 Upper thermostat
12 Anode rod
13 Dip tube
14 Lower element
15 Lower thermostat
16 Draincock
17 Bracket
18 Element flange
19 Gasket

Loose Wires

Remove the access panels for both heating elements and check for wires that may have loosened from the terminals. If a wire is loose or disconnected, turn off the power to the heater, loosen the terminal screw, bend the end of the wire around it, and tighten the screw.

Defective Thermostat Element

To determine if the problem is in the element, thermostat, or high-limit protector, test each part with a volt ohmmeter (VOM). If you don't have a VOM, try simple logic. If the heater produces plenty of warm water but no hot water, the top element of the thermostat is probably defective. If you get a few gallons of very hot water followed by cool water, the bottom element or thermostat probably needs to be replaced. Since elements fail much more often than thermostats, assume a faulty element or test with a VOM.

How to Replace an Element

■ Shut off power and water supply to heater.

■ Drain tank to below element to be replaced.

■ Disconnect wires to terminals and unscrew element.

■ Pull element straight out of tank.

■ Clean gasket surface, coat lightly with pipe-joint compound, and seat a new gasket.

■ Attach new element to heater and reconnect wires to terminals.

■ Before turning on power, fill tank with water (an element that is energized when dry will burn out in seconds).

■ Bleed all trapped air through faucets.

■ Replace insulation, thermostat protection plates, and access panel.

■ Turn on power.

After 45 minutes if there's no hot water, a replacement thermostat is in order.

How to Replace a Thermostat

- Turn off the power.

- Disconnect the wires from the thermostat's terminals.

- Pry out the old thermostat and snap the new one into the clip.

- Reconnect the wires.

- Replace the insulation.

- Turn on the power.

- Allow both elements to complete their heating cycles and then test water temperature at the faucets using a meat thermometer.

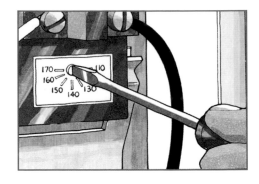

▲ Adjust the temperature with a screwdriver.

- Adjust the thermostat with a screwdriver until the water temperature is between 130 and 140 degrees Fahrenheit.

Clearing Drains

Soap, hair, food particles, and cooking grease all clog drainage lines. Minimize your chances of developing blockages by restricting what goes down the drain. Never flush paper products, other than toilet tissue, down the drain. Put soap wrappers, facial tissues, and feminine-hygiene products into a wastebasket for disposal. Don't pour grease down the kitchen drain, and unless you have a garbage disposal, avoid letting small bits of food fall into the drain. When using the garbage disposal, let the water run long enough so that all food residue is flushed completely into the main drain line.

Occasionally a fixture trap will accumulate a blockage that can be forced clear with an ordinary plunger or compressed air. Most blockages build up inside pipes over time and must be cleared with a drain auger, or "snake." The method you choose to clear a drain will depend on the fixture involved and the size of the drainage line.

USING A PLUNGER IN FIXTURE TRAPS

Plungers and cans of compressed air can free simple trapped clogs. When forcing a clog from a fixture's trap using a plunger (or compressed air), be sure to plug any connecting airways. When plunging a lavatory, for example, use a wet rag to plug the overflow hole in the basin. When forcing the trap of a two-compartment sink, plug the opposite drain. After the debris has been forced from the trap and into the drain line, run very hot water through the line to move the clog to the main stack or soil pipe.

▲ The trap on the sink fixture must be removed so that a snake can be put directly into the drainpipe.

SNAKING FIXTURE DRAINS

In order to use an auger or snake on a fixture such as a sink, the trap must first be removed so the cable can be inserted directly into the drainpipe. Remove the trap with a pipe wrench or adjustable pliers by loosening the nuts at the top of the trap and at the drain connection near the wall. With S-traps, loosen the nuts near the floor and at the trap. To avoid breaking or crackling a chrome P-trap, hold it firmly and turn the nut with steady, even pressure. After the trap is removed, insert the corkscrew-like head of the snake or auger into the drainpipe until it reaches the blockage. Clamp the cranked handle onto the other end and turn it to rotate the head and engage the blockage. Push and pull the auger until the pipe is clear.

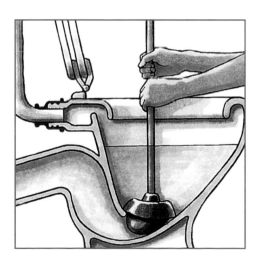

▲ Plug the overflow hole in a basin before attempting to use a plunger on the drain.

SNAKING A SHOWER

To snake a tub, remove the coverplate from the overflow valve and push the head of the cable into the overflow pipe. This is easier than working through the drain opening. Rotate the head of the auger and engage the blockage, as noted above.

If drain water backs up into the tub or shower from another fixture, it probably means that the main sewer line is clogged and snaking the shower will most likely be ineffective.

CLEARING A TOILET

Try to force the clog with a plunger. A plunger with a collapsible funnel works best. If plunging doesn't do the trick, remove the water from the bowl and use a small mirror and a flashlight to look up into the trap. If you can see the obstruction—often a toothpaste cap, hairpin, or comb—chances are you can reach it with a wire hook.

If all else fails, you can rent a closet auger and crank the auger through the trap several times. The auger's cable is just long enough to reach the toilet flange, at the toilet's base. As you pull the cable out of the trap, keep cranking the handle.

a) Use an auger to clear toilet blockages if b) a plunger doesn't do the job.

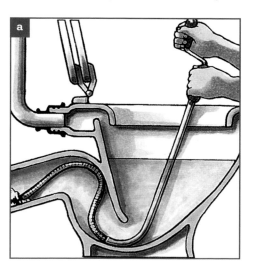
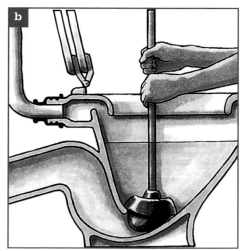

SNAKING A SEWER LINE

You can rent a sewer-cleaning machine, but before you do, get several bids from drain cleaning companies. Often they can do the job for little more than the cost of the rental. Most sewer clogs are the result of collapsed pipes or entangled tree roots and are best left to a professional.

7

Accessible and Safe Living

Whether a family member is dealing with a disability or aging, creating a barrier-free environment means not only increased physical well-being but also the sense of empowerment that comes with the freedom to go about one's daily routine.

Most homes are simply not designed for people with reduced mobility. Structural adaptations such as ramps, widened doorways, enhanced fixtures, and the like are best undertaken with the guidance of a reputable contractor. On the other hand, smaller, less complicated changes to accessories such as faucets, cabinet pulls, and lighting can be accomplished by most do-it-yourselfers.

NOTE: In an effort to break down the barriers individuals with disabilities confront in employment and public accommodations, Congress passed the Americans with Disabilities Act (ADA), which is enforced by the Civil Rights Division of the U.S. Department of Justice. The ADA's Standards for Accessible Design set guidelines in the design of, construction of, or alteration to commercial facilities to accommodate individuals with disabilities. Although adherence to the ADA's Accessibilities Guidelines (ADAAG) is not required in private residences, reputable architects and contractors will be familiar with and mindful of them when making alterations for accessibility in a private home.

In the Kitchen

Consider making the kitchen as accessible as possible when planning a new construction or remodeling an existing home. The following adaptations can make any kitchen more accommodating to individuals with restricted mobility:

- Install a single-lever kitchen faucet that allows control of both water volume and temperature.

- Replace pull-knob cabinet doors or drawer hardware with D-shaped handles.

- Install bright task lighting over the sink and cook top areas.

- Countertops may be uncomfortably high for an individual seated in a wheelchair; either lower them or install pull-out shelves beneath the counter.

- Lower cupboard height.

- Be sure countertops and vinyl floor covering are in contrasting colors so the edge of the countertop stands out clearly.

- A cooktop with offset front and back burners will eliminate the need to reach over a hot front burner to get to the back burner.

- A side-by-side refrigerator/freezer is the most accessible style for an individual seated in a wheelchair.

- Install numerous ground fault circuit interrupter (GFCI) receptacles at convenient heights.

▲ A single-lever faucet is easier to turn on and off.

Making Bathrooms Safer

Bathrooms are used frequently throughout the day, and getting in and out of tubs and showers requires some precarious moves. This can make a bathroom a frustrating and even dangerous place for people with restricted mobility. As human beings live longer, more consideration must be given to making bathroom facilities safer and more accommodating as we age. Contractors and architects familiar with the Americans with Disabilities Act Accessibility Guidelines can help determine the type of adaptation required in remodeling or new constructions. The extent of the adaptations will depend on whether the family member needs assistance from a caregiver to go about his or her daily routine or—although reduced in mobility—simply needs assistive devices to continue independent living.

Safe and accessible bathrooms should be designed with the following considerations.

▶ All bathrooms should be equipped with grab bars.

GRAB BARS

Bathtubs, shower stalls, and toilets should be equipped with grab bars mounted to the floor or wall. Grab bars in and next to the tub help family members maintain balance both in and out of the tub. Grab bars on both sides of the toilet provide more assured maneuvering. Grab bars can be anchored to the walls or attached, as add-on items, to the front edge of the bathtub. If you install the wall-mounted grab bars, be sure that the screws are anchored into wood studs or framing.

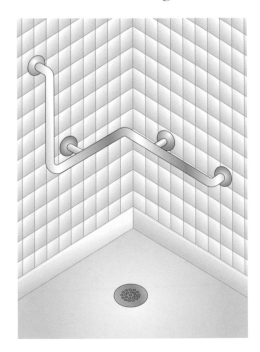

TUB SEATS

A tub seat can provide stability in a shower stall or bathtub. If the tub seat is used in a bathtub, a flexible hose with showerhead attachment eliminates the need for immersion.

WALK-IN TUBS/ROLL-IN SHOWERS

Designed to eliminate the need for the user to climb into and out of the tub, walk-ins permit same-level passage from floor to tub. Roll-in showers are wide enough to accommodate a wheelchair.

NONSKID FLOORING

Look for nonskid tiles when remodeling bathroom floors. Use nonskid mats and place no-slip decals on the bottom of tubs and shower stalls.

SINGLE-LEVER FAUCET

Install a single-lever faucet that allows control of both water volume and temperature.

▼ Walkin tubs and roll-in showers are now readily available.

ANTISCALD DEVICE

Adjust your water heater to 120 degrees Fahrenheit or less and install an antiscald device that automatically prevents water from becoming too hot.

The kitchen and bathroom are not the only places in the home in which accessibility is an important issue. Front doors, stairs, and hallways can be made safer for people of all ages and of varying levels of mobility.

▲ Thresholds should be at least 32 inches wide.

Front Door

According to the AARP (an advocacy group for people over 50), a front-door width of at least 32 inches will make passage easier. A 32-inch width will allow an individual in a wheelchair or using a walker to gain entrance comfortably. Lever-type door handles eliminate the need to grasp and turn and may be helpful to those suffering from arthritis or any other movement-restricting condition. A person in a wheelchair or on crutches needs a clear space of at least 18 inches next to the door handle in order to get close enough to operate it. Time-delayed door closers and/or a keyless locking system can also help.

Personal safety in and around the front entrance is important. Motion sensor lighting provides instant illumination to negotiate steps, lock or unlock the door, and eliminate the cover most intruders use to gain entry. Keep shrubs and greenery cut back around the entrance to your home to dissuade someone from hiding there. The AARP also recommends that you get in the habit of using an entrance that is visible from the street or from a neighbor's perspective rather than one hidden from view.

Stairs and Hallways

Stairs and hallways should be kept free of clutter, toys, laundry baskets, or any of the typical items that seem to accumulate there. Make sure stairs and hallways are well lighted: switches should be installed at the top and the bottom of the stairs to prevent climbing up or down simply to turn the light on or off. Properly anchored railings should be installed on all stairs; consider railings in hallways for family members who are infirm.

THE AARP'S CHECKLIST FOR STAIR SAFETY INCLUDES THE FOLLOWING TIPS:

- Treads are 11 to 12 inches deep and 36 inches wide.
- The staircase has one landing for every ten steps.
- Between each landing there are at least three steps.
- When the staircase changes direction, there is a landing.
- Handrails are installed on both sides of the staircase.

STAIR CONSTRUCTION

Staircase dimensions and designs are strictly controlled by building codes, which govern such measurements as tread size and shape, rise and run, minimum headroom, handrail position, and spacing of balusters. Consult your local building department before building or remodeling any staircase.

HANDRAILS

Handrails are required on staircases according to building codes. If the staircase is narrower than 40 inches, only one handrail is needed. Staircases wider than 40 inches require two handrails. Staircases with tapered treads or winders must have a handrail on the side where the tread is widest. If the widest part of the tread occurs against the wall, two handrails are needed: one on the wall and one as part of the balustrade. The end of the handrail should extend beyond the top and the bottom of the stairs.

Handrails can help you keep your balance, but to protect from

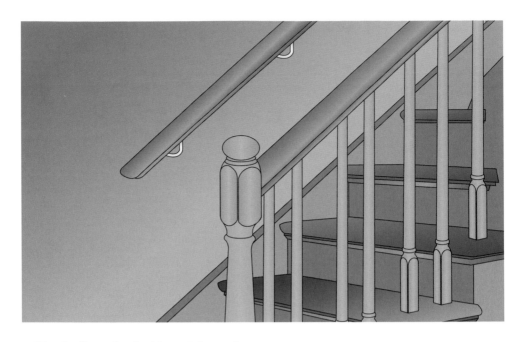

▲ Handrails on both sides of the stairs offer extra protection.

injury in case of a fall, any handrail must be strong and securely anchored enough to support an adult's weight. Most building codes state that a handrail should be at least 30 inches but no more than 36 inches above the treads. Standard handrail diameter is 1⅝ inches, large enough to support an adult's weight but small enough that the hand can completely encircle the rail to grip it securely.

The screws holding handrail brackets must be anchored into wall studs and must be long enough to pass though the bracket base and the plaster or wallboard—a total of to 1 inch of material—before they reach the studs. Screws must be at least 2 inches long in order to penetrate the solid wood base. If the bracket screws do not penetrate at least 1 inch into the wood stud, replace them with longer screws.

Ramps

The construction of a ramp enabling individuals in wheelchairs or using walkers or crutches to circumvent stairs is best left to an experienced contractor familiar with the Americans with Disabilities Act Accessibilities Guidelines (ADAAG). Although the technical requirements outlined in the ADAAG are intended for construction in public buildings, a responsible contractor will adhere to those standards when building a ramp for use in a private home. The following are some of the minimum requirements for the construction of a ramp intended for use by individuals in wheelchairs as outlined in the ADAAG:

- Ramps must be at least 36 inches wide.

- Railings on both sides of the ramp are recommended.

- Railings should be between 34 and 38 inches high.

- Both ends of handrails should extend 12 inches beyond the edge of the ramp.

- The rise (or slope) between landings should be no more than 30 inches.

- Every 30 feet of ramp requires a 5-foot by 5-foot landing

- Landings should be placed at the top, bottom, and all switchbacks (turns) in the ramp.

- The surface of the ramp should be of nonslip material.

- Curbs, walls, or edge protectors at least 2 inches high on the edges of the ramp prevent the wheels of the chair from slipping off.

Preventing Falls

According to the National Safety Council, slips and falls cause more hospital admissions, injuries, and deaths to older adults than any other mishap or malady. The changes that occur as we age often contribute to the act of falling and to the injury sustained. But there are ways that we can make ourselves stronger, and our homes safer, so that slips and falls are not inevitable.

KEEP YOUR BODY STRONG

Stay fit. Work with a physician to establish an exercise program designed especially for you. It is particularly important to maintain muscle mass and flexibility.

Consider diet and nutrition; calcium-rich foods should be a staple of your diet.

Wear prescribed eyeglasses and hearing aides and have your eyes and ears checked regularly for any changes.

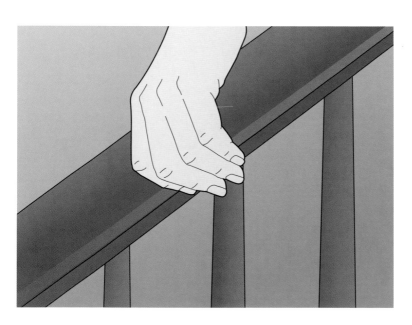

▲ Slips and falls are the most common cause of injury to older Americans.

Educate yourself about the medications prescribed to you. Find out whether side effects include dizziness or disorientation and inquire about alternatives.

No more than two alcoholic beverages should be consumed a day.

Stop smoking.

THINK AND ACT SAFELY

Don't leap out of bed or up from the sofa. Sit for a moment and allow your blood pressure to stabilize before standing.

Temperature affects the body. Monitor temperatures in your home so you are not too hot or cold.

Use assistive devices such as a cane or walker if you feel dizzy or unsteady when walking.

Arrange items in cabinets to avoid having to reach for them. If you must reach items high on the shelf, use a proper stepladder with handrails.

Wear flat, comfortable shoes with nonskid soles. Avoid wearing flimsy slippers or socks on wood or tile surfaces that can be slippery.

CHANGES IN THE HOME

Eliminate area rugs in high-traffic areas such as hallways, at the bottom or top of stairs, and on tile, slate, or marble floors at entry doors.

If you must have area rugs, be sure they have nonslip backing material or are firmly attached to the floor.

Stair treads should be kept well lit and clear of debris. If you choose to carpet treads, select a firm, thin pad and tightly woven carpet. (Thick padding and carpet will interfere with firm footing.)

Keep floors free of clutter, electrical cords, and telephone and cable wires.

Provide sufficient space to move freely throughout the home; pathways should be at least 32 inches wide and free of jutting furniture and obstacles on the floor.

Rooms should be well lit, with ample wall switches that allow you to turn off the light as you leave the room.

A telephone and a light within easy reach of the bed are prudent and provide a sense of well-being.

Pharmaceutical Safety

People over 65 years of age consume more prescription drugs and over-the-counter (OTC) medicines than any other age group—according to the National Institute on Aging (NIA)—and while such substances can increase life span and help us to live more comfortably, they should be administered with utmost care. Whether you are taking medication yourself or acting as caregiver to another, precautions are in order when a physician's prescription, OTCs, vitamins, minerals, and/or herbal and dietary supplements are taken. The National Institute on Aging has some prudent recommendations for the safe use of medicines.

USING MEDICINES SAFELY

- Keep a list of all the prescription and OTC medications you take; review the list frequently with your physician and pharmacist.

- Ask for larger type on the label of your medication if you have trouble reading it.

- Read the label on prescribed medication to ensure that it was written for you.

- Read and follow all directions on medicines, including the amount and schedule your doctor prescribes.

- Dispose of medicine that has reached its expiration date. (Flush it down the toilet.)

- Consult with your doctor if medications don't seem to be working; don't stop taking medications without first speaking with your physician.

- Ask your doctor about side effects and what to expect when taking medications.

- Never consume medication prescribed to someone else.

- Alcohol should not be consumed with medication unless approved by your doctor.

- Install bright, task lighting in the bathroom, or wherever you will be reading or taking prescriptions.

- Dispose of any pill or capsule that you drop on the floor.

- Keep all medicine away from children.

Older Drivers

For most of us, driving means freedom. The ability to get in the car and go means that you don't have to deal with the vagaries of others, the timetables of public transportation, the expense of a taxi. Although being older doesn't cause accidents, the act of aging can affect driving. Changes in vision and the ability to react, health issues, and the presence of certain medications can all affect our ability to handle an automobile safely, according to the National Institute on Aging. The NIA's Age Page on older drivers provides helpful information on such issues as improving driving skills and how to decide whether to stop driving entirely, and includes the following advice.

▼ Make sure the type on prescription labels is large enough for you to read.

Improve Driving

DO SOME PLANNING

Before getting in the car, think about the route you will take. Take streets familiar to you and limit distractions such as the radio, conversation, or interior noises like fans. Avoid driving conditions that are difficult for you such as night driving, rush hour, and inclement weather. Plan all trips when you believe traffic will be at its thinnest: weekdays and between 10 a.m. and 2 p.m. during the day.

DRIVE DEFENSIVELY

Put a great deal of space between your vehicle and the car in front of you. Resist taking risks when yielding, turning, changing lanes, or passing other vehicles. Educate yourself about the driving regulations in your state. Avoid getting behind the wheel if you are under stress or are tired.

TAKE A DRIVING CLASS

Driver refresher courses are offered by the AARP (American Association of Retired Persons) and the AAA (American Automobile Association) and may even reduce your auto insurance premiums on completion.

GET EXTRA FEATURES

Power steering and brakes, automatic transmission, and large rearview mirrors make driving more efficient and easier. Light-colored cars are more visible to other drivers. Driving with the headlights on at all times will also help other drivers to see you. A clean windshield and headlights, properly functioning wiper blades, and a rear-window defroster can all contribute to increased visibility.

Whether to Stop Driving

The decision to stop driving a vehicle should not be made based on age but on such issues as one's health, genes, lifestyle, and sense of confidence. Since we all age differently there exists no magic number at which a driver's license should be relinquished. Consider the following statements, and if any are applicable to you, you should consider giving up driving.

- You are frequently lost even on roads once familiar to you.
- Drivers of other vehicles often honk or gesture at you.
- You've recently had a fender bender or two.
- You are often surprised by the sudden appearance of other vehicles or pedestrians.
- Family members have voiced concern about your driving.
- You drive as infrequently as possible due to a lack of confidence.

Since the decision to stop driving is not an easy one, consider contacting the AARP at www.aarp.org or AAA at www.aaa.com to obtain publications to help with your assessment.

Getting Around without Your Car

Even without a car, there are still options for getting around in most communities. Contact local organizations dedicated to serving senior citizens to inquire about transportation services. There may be low-cost public transportation available to those who are 65 or older.

Religious, social or nonprofit organizations may offer transportation services to senior citizens. Keep in mind that operating a car is expensive, and without the monthly cost of fuel and maintenance, more funds may be available to you to pay for taxis or hired drivers.

Roofing

Inspection

The roof plays an integral role in protecting a house and in so doing is exposed to ultraviolet radiation, extreme weather conditions, moisture, and the possible infestation of insects. Penetrating moisture and boring insects can seriously damage a roof's structural members. An annual inspection of the roof, from both inside and out, should be every homeowner's priority.

INSIDE INSPECTION

If your house has an unfinished attic, inspect the inside of the roof armed with a good source of light. In general, you are looking for any sign of a leak, insect damage, or structural sagging. Water stains on interior framing may be a sign of weakness in the roofing material. Check the roof sheathing, which is a felt-like material hung between the rafters.

Carefully inspect the flashing, or the areas on the roof where there are joints, such as at dormer windows, at vent stacks, or where roof planes meet. Pay special attention to openings in the roof such as plumbing vents and

chimneys; water could be entering around them. If your roof is finished with slate or clay tile, sunlight will be revealed through any cracked or broken tiles.

ROOF MATERIALS

Asphalt Shingles
- Relatively low cost
- Easy to apply and repair
- Wood and paper or fiberglass construction (fiberglass is the most fire-resistant)
- 20-year life expectancy
- Most commonly offered in 3-tab construction

Slate or Clay Tiles
- Beautiful but high maintenance
- Long-lived: 100 years or more
- Expensive to install, repair, or renew

Wood Shingles or Shakes
- Commonly made of cedar or pine
- Can deteriorate if not properly installed
- Between 15 and 40-year lifeline
- Become brittle as they age

OUTSIDE INSPECTION

If you are uncomfortable on a ladder, inspect the roof from the ground, using a pair of binoculars.

Check for missing, curled, or cracked asphalt shingles. Look into roof gutters or under gutter downspouts for excess granule deposits, a sure sign of deteriorating shingles.

Misaligned slate or clay tiles will stand out against the straight lines of the others. Differences in color are also a sign that a tile has become dislodged or is loose and has shifted position.

Inspect a wood-shingled roof from the ground, checking for cracked or broken shingles. If you go onto the roof, be particularly careful not to inflict more damage, since wood shingles become more brittle with age. Shingles are more pliable after a good rain, but this will also make the roof more slippery.

On roofs of all finishing materials, inspect flashing at vents, wall joints, chimneys, plumbing stacks, dormers, skylights, along rakes and eaves, and at any valleys. Make sure the seal of roofing cement or caulking at the edge of the flashing material is intact. Flashing material, usually galvanized metal—and the compound that seals it—prevents water from penetrating the house along joints and should be frequently inspected and maintained. Inspect all areas where the flashing material meets brick to ensure that mortar has not separated from metal flashing.

▼ Flashing components to inspect yearly:

1 Chimney	6 Along the rakes
2 Vent stack	7 Eaves
3 Wall	8 Over windows
4 Dormer	9 Over doors
5 Where roofplanes meet at valleys	

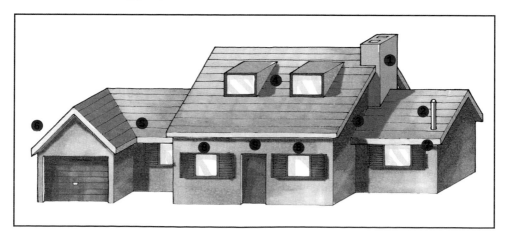

Gutters

Gutters are an all-important part of the preventive maintenance of your home as they direct water away from the roof, walls, and foundation of the building. The varied materials from which gutters are made have advantages and disadvantages. Wood gutters of fir, redwood, or cedar can last the lifetime of the house if maintained, and are strong and attractive, particularly when paired with wood shingles. Galvanized steel, while low in cost, requires regular painting with special, peel-resistant primer. Aluminum gutters offer homeowners a wide choice of colors and resist corrosion but bend easily under the weight of a ladder. Vinyl gutters are perhaps the easiest to install and offer the same wide range of colors that aluminum ones do.

KEEP GUTTERS CLEAN

Gutters should be cleared after leaves have fallen in both autumn and in early spring. You'll need a ladder, heavy work gloves, a rag, a piece of plastic or sheet metal cut to fit the interior shape of the gutter, a whisk broom, a garden hose and source of water, a trowel, and a bucket.

- Stuff a rag into the drop outlet of the gutter to prevent debris from lodging there.

- Wearing gloves and using a piece of plastic or metal, scrape debris along the inside of the gutter, removing it with the garden trowel and disposing of it in a bucket suspended from the ladder.

- Whisk out the gutter using the broom and remove the rag blocking the outlet.

- Flush water through the gutter from the hose.

- Inspect the water drains to make sure water is running through efficiently.

- If standing pools of water remain, check for leaking gutter seams or clogged downspouts, and repair seams or free downspouts using a snake or drain auger.

LEAF STRAINER

Homes that are heavily wooded or those with recurring blocked downspouts may benefit from the installation of leaf strainers in the gutter outlets. Another alternative is to install wire guards that run the length of the gutters.

▲ a) Leaf strainers and b) wire guards can protect gutters from an accumulation of debris.

SNOW AND ICE REMOVAL

Heavy snow and ice can sag or break gutters if they accumulate in large amounts. Use a broom to knock blockages free from an upstairs window or from a ladder. If gutters are continually clogged with snow, install a snow board of treated wood that runs parallel to the gutter along the edge of the roof. A piece of 1-inch by 3-inch lumber, bolted to the roof with steel brackets, prevents the snow from collecting in the gutter.

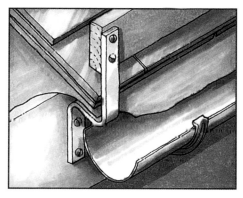

▲ Excess snow and ice can be deflected with snow boards.

Preventing Storm Damage

There are steps you can take to make your roof more wind-resistant. If you are starting from scratch with the roof sheathing, the first line of defense against leaks is an underlayment course of 30-pound felt paper. Although more costly and trickier to install than 15-pound, its thicker base resists tearing. To secure the felt, opt for metal washers or disks and galvanized nails as opposed to staples. Choose interlocking shingles or shingles with self-adhesive strips for greater wind resistance. Use galvanized roofing nails to install asphalt shingles, longer nails if you are placing a second layer of shingle over an existing layer.

If you live in an area where high winds or wind storms are common, you may suffer wind damage to the roof despite every precaution. Keep a roll of 6-mil plastic or a large plastic tarp handy to temporarily cover the roof should damage occur. Purchase the plastic before the arrival of a storm or the ensuing damage since emergency materials are difficult to find (due to increased demand) in the days following a major storm.

Leaks

Annual roof inspections and routine maintenance can help prevent the troublesome and costly effects of a leak. Most leaks are caused when water penetrates the roof from an external opening. Broken gutters, leaking downspouts, broken or missing shingles, and damaged flashing material may result in water being admitted to the home's interior. The position of the damp area on the ceiling or wall may help you determine where moisture is penetrating, but since water will seek the lowest point, it may penetrate at a higher level and then run down.

▲ **Some causes of penetrating moisture:**
1 Broken gutter
2 Leaking downspouts
3 Missing shingles
4 Damaged flashing
5 Loose shingles

COMMON ROOF LEAKS AND HOW TO STOP THEM!

■ Moist spots on wall near ceiling in upstairs rooms: Most likely rainwater has overflowed at the joint of a blocked gutter and is penetrating the wall below it. You should clear debris from the gutter and repair any damaged joints.

■ A wet spot in isolation, halfway up the wall: A cracked downspout, possibly blocked with debris, introduces water to the wall behind the leak. Repair the crack after removing debris. Use stain-blocking primer on the wall behind the downspout and finish with a coat of exterior paint.

■ During or after a heavy rainfall, moist patches collect on the ceiling in an upstairs room: A broken roof shingle permits water entry. Replace damaged shingle.

■ Wet areas or water dripping from the roof ridge to wall, or around a vent, chimney, or exhaust fan: The flashing around roof joints may be damaged or the sealant around the flashing may be deteriorated. Replace flashing or cover affected area with plastic roof cement.

WET ATTIC INSULATION

The water from a roof leak can soak through to the attic insulation, decreasing the efficiency of the insulation and causing mildew, mold, or damage to the ceiling below. As soon as the roof has been mended and the leak stopped, take steps to dry out the attic insulation.

Wearing a dust mask and protective goggles, pull the wet insulation away from the affected area and remove any standing water on the plaster or wallboard ceiling. Mop up the water with sponge and pail, or use a wet/dry vacuum. You can also drain the water through the ceiling by drilling small holes. (See "Ceiling Damage" section, facing page.)

Next, dry out the insulation by ventilating the attic. Open any windows, turn on the power ventilator if you have one, or set up numerous portable house fans throughout the attic. When all moisture has been removed, replace insulation. For blown fiberglass, use a leaf rake to gather and respread insulation.

Ceiling Damage

REMOVE STANDING WATER IMMEDIATELY

If water from a roof leak is permitted to stand and soak through the ceiling, widespread and expensive damage can be the result. To minimize or eliminate water damage to the plaster or wallboard, go into the attic, pull back the insulation between the joists, and find out where puddles of water have formed. If water has been standing long enough, you will see wet spots on the ceiling from the finished side. To remove the water, create a drain hole in the ceiling with a cordless drill and _-inch bit or a hammer and nail. Place a bucket on a ladder under the hole to catch the draining water.

After the water is removed and the roof has been repaired, drain holes can be patched and painted.

WATER STAINS

Stains on ceilings are often the product of a roof leak. After the water has been drained and the cause of the leak repaired, sand the area of the stain well and then apply a coat of fast-drying sealer. Interior wall paint can be then be applied over the sealer without the stain bleeding through.

REPAIRING A DRYWALL CEILING

The difficulty of the repair will depend, of course, on the severity of the damage. Minor damage can be repaired rather simply with drywall compound, after the affected area has entirely dried.

PATCHING A HOLE IN A DRYWALL CEILING

- Before beginning work on any repair, turn off the circuit that supplies electricity to the area. Widen the hole at the center of the damaged area with a hammer so that you can check for electrical wiring and the position of ceiling joists. Use a flashlight and mirror to examine the area for wiring.

- After determining that the area is free of wiring, pencil in a square or rectangle encompassing the affected area. Cut out the square of damaged drywall using a utility knife or drywall saw. Two sides of the opening should back up to the nearest joists.

- The parallel sides of the two existing joists will act as a nailing surface for furring strips, but you will need to create a nailing surface for the top and bottom edges of the cutout. You can do this by toenailing 2 × 4 blocking between the joists and at each end of the cutout. Extend the blocking at least halfway beyond the cut ends of the existing drywall to act as a nailing surface for the new piece of drywall.

- Nail 1 × 2 furring strips flush to the bottom edges of the joists.

- Using drywall of the same thickness, cut a piece to fit the opening; there should be a ⅛ inch gap around it when it is placed within the hole. Drive nails into the patch and through to the blocking and furring. Place wallboard tape over the cracks and finish the area with wallboard compound. Sand the area after the compound has dried.

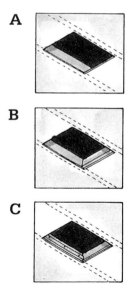

▲ Patching a hole in drywall ceiling
A Cut out a square of damaged area.
B Toenail 2 × 4 blocking between joists.
C Nail in 1 × 2 furring strips.

REPAIRING A PLASTER CEILING

■ Obtaining a good bond between the lath (wooden strips beneath the plaster) and the plaster is imperative. To ensure this, apply several thin coats of plaster and create a rough surface between coats.

■ Remove the damaged or loose plaster from the affected area. Make sure that the lath to which the plaster will be applied is in sound condition. Before applying plaster, either dampen the lath and plaster edges with water or use a bonding liquid to prepare it. (This will prevent cracks in the patch.)

■ Apply a thin undercoat of plaster, pressing it firmly into the lath, and scratch the surface before it sets. You can use a nail or the edge of a trowel to striate the surface. Apply a second coating of plaster and scratch before it sets. Apply a finish coat after the second coat has dried. Sand lightly when the third coat has dried.

◀ Repairing a plaster ceiling

A Apply a thin undercoat of plaster.
B Apply a finish coat after the second coat has dried.

Ladder Safety

The decision to work on a ladder—either to make roof inspections or to perform simple household tasks—is a personal one. If you decide to engage in work requiring the use of a ladder, be sure to conform to the safety guidelines offered by the U.S. Consumer Product Safety Commission.

■ Do not exceed the maximum load rating of the ladder in use.

■ Use a ladder high enough for the job: a minimum of 3 feet should extend beyond the surface work area (roofline).

■ Never use a metal ladder around power lines or electrical wiring; a metal ladder will pose the risk of electric shock.

■ Extension or straight ladders should be placed on a firm surface and be tilted at a 75-degree angle.

■ Metal ladders should have rubber-capped feet to prevent slippage.

■ Make sure the legs on stepladders are fully extended and locked into place.

■ Extension ladders have locking devices; make sure they are engaged on both sides.

■ For an extra measure of protection, have an assistant hold the bottom of the ladder steady.

■ Always block a door before setting up a ladder in front of it.

■ Stay centered while working on a ladder; don't lean to the side.

■ Never use the top step or fold-out tray of the ladder as a step.

■ Stow ladders away after use.

▼ Consider purchasing a ladder specially designed for the roof if you plan to work there.

WEIGHT CAPACITY (USER PLUS MATERIALS) RATINGS FOR LADDERS

- Type I—Industrial/Heavy Duty: User plus materials capacity of no more than 250 pounds

- Type II—Commercial/Medium Duty: User plus materials capacity of no more than 225 pounds

- Type III—Household/Light Duty: User plus materials capacity of no more than 200 pounds

- When purchasing a ladder match the user's weight, plus any repair materials he or she will be carrying, to the weight capacity of the ladder. Ladders should be tested and labeled by Underwriters Laboratories.

- If you decide to work on your roof, consider purchasing a roof ladder, which is specially designed for working in that environment.

Sources

American Academy of
Pediatrics

AARP (Formerly American
Association of Retired
Persons)

AAA (www.aaa.com)

American Red Cross

American SIDS Institute

California Attorney General's
Office, Crime and Violence
Prevention Center

Canada Safety Council

Center for Universal Design,
North Carolina State
University

City of Minneapolis and
Minneapolis Police
(www.ci.minneapolis
.mn.us/police/crime-
prevention)

Electrical Safety Foundation
International

Familydoctor.org

Federal Emergency
Management Agency (FEMA)
(www.fema.gov)

Federal Trade Commission
(www.consumer.gov/idtheft)

Home Fire Sprinkler Coalition

Insurance Information
Institute (www.iii.org)

MedicineNet.com

MSN House & Home/Roofing

National AG Safety Database

National Crime Prevention
Council

National Electrical Safety
Foundation

National Fire Protection
Association

National Flood Insurance
Program (NFIP)

National Institute on Aging
(NIA) (www.nia.nih.gov)

National Safe Kids Campaign

National Safety Council

National Oceanic and
Atmospheric Administration
(NOAA)

National Weather Service

Nemours Foundation
(KidsHealth)

The New York Times
(Personal Health, 7/13/04
Your Home, 6/13/04)

Popular Mechanics Complete
How-To

SIDS Network

Underwriters Laboratories

U.S. Access Board, Atlanta
Research and Education
Foundation

U.S. Consumer Products
Safety Commission
(www.cpsc.gov)

U.S. Department of Housing
and Urban Development
(HUD)

U.S. Department of Justice,
Civil Rights Division
(www.usdoj.gov/crd/ada)

U.S. Department of Justice,
Bureau of Justice Statistics

U.S. Environmental Protection
Agency (EPA)

U.S. Fire Administration
(www.usfa.fema.gov)

Washington State Department
of Health, Crib Safety

WebMD.com

Index